Pension Systems in the European Union: Competition and Tax Aspects

EFS Brochure Series

1. Harmonization of Company Taxation in the European Community
Some Comments on the Ruding Committee Report
Lans Bovenberg, Sijbren Cnossen, F J GM Vanistendael, J W B Westerburgen

2. Taxation of Cross-Border Income, Harmonization, and Tax Neutrality under European Community Law - An Institutional Approach
Klaus Vogel, Johan Brands, Kees van Raad

3. Neutrality and Subsidiarity in Taxation
Stephen Smith, René Barents

4. Towards a Dual Income Tax?
Scandinavian and Austrian Experiences
Leif Muten, Peter B. Sørensen, Kåre P. Hagen, Bernd Genser

5. Taxpayer Protection in the European Union
Dirk Albregtse, Henk van Arendonk (Eds)

6. Selected Issues in European Tax Law: The Legal Character of VAT and the Application of General Principles of Justice
Dirk Albregtse, Han Kogels (Eds)

7. Pension Systems in the European Union: Competition and Tax Aspects
Leo Stevens, Humbert Drabbe, Gerry Dietvorst, Peter Kavelaars

Pension Systems in the European Union: Competition and Tax Aspects

Authors

Leo Stevens
Humbert Drabbe
Gerry Dietvorst
Peter Kavelaars

Foundation for European Fiscal Studies
Erasmus University Rotterdam

KLUWER LAW INTERNATIONAL
THE HAGUE - LONDON - BOSTON

Published by
Kluwer Law International Ltd
Sterling House
66 Wilton Road
London SW1V 1DE
United Kingdom

Sold and distributed
in the USA and Canada by
Kluwer Law International
675 Massachusetts Avenue
Cambridge MA 02139
USA

Kluwer Law International incorporates
the publishing programmes of
Graham & Trotman Ltd
Kluwer Law & Taxation Publishers
and Martinus Nijhoff Publishers

In all other countries sold and distributed by
Kluwer Law International
PO Box 85889
2508 CN The Hague
The Netherlands

ISBN 90-411-9752-4

First published 1999

British Library Cataloguing in Publication Data
A catalogue record for this book is available from the British Library

Typeset in 10/11pt Palatino by RTR Information Design, London.
Printed and bound in Great Britain by Selwood Printing Ltd, Burgess Hill, West Sussex.

Contents

List of Tables

Appendix A

List of Abbreviations

ABP	Algemein Burgelÿk Pensioenfunds (Public Servants Superannuation Fund)
ALM	Asset/liability management
AOW	Algemene Ouderdomswet (Public old-age insurance)
ATS	Austrian Schilling
BEF	Belgian Franc
bn	billion
BNB	*Beslissingen in Nederlandse Belastingzaken* (Journal for Dutch Tax Jurisprudence)
CEA	*Comité Européen des Assurances* (European Committee of Insurers)
CHF	Swiss Franc
Commission	European Commission
DEM	Deutschmark
DKK	Danish Crown
EASDAQ	European Association of Security Dealers Automated Quotation
EC	European Community/European Communities
ECJ	Court of Justice of the European Community
ECR	Report of Cases before the Court of Justice and the Court of First Instance
ECU	European Currency Unity
EEC	European Economic Community
EFRP	European Federation for Retirement Provision
EMU	European Monetary Union
EU	European Union
FFSA	*Fédération Française des Sociétés d'Assurance* (French Federation of Insurance Companies)
FIM	Finnish Markka
FOR	*Fiscale Oudedagsreserve* (Dutch pension allowance for the self-employed)
FRF	French Franc
GBP	British Pound
GDP	Gross Domestic Product
n.a.	not available

NLG	Dutch Guilder
NOK	Norwegian Crown
NSV	*Nederlands Standaard Verdrag* (Dutch Model Tax Treaty)
OECD	Organisation for Economic Cooperation and Development
OJ EC	*Official Journal of the European Community*
PAYG	Pay-as-you-go
RSV	*Rechtspraak Sociale Verzekering* (Journal for Dutch Social Security Cases)
SC	Supreme Court
SERPS	State Earnings-Related Pension Scheme
Stb	Wederlands Staatblad (Dutch Official Journal)
UN	United Nations
V-N	*Vakstudie-Nieuws* (Dutch Weekly for Tax Affairs)
WAO	Wet arbeids ongeschiktheids ver zehering (Invalidity Insurance Act for Employees)
WAZ	Wet arbeids ongeschiktheids ver zehering zelfstandigin (Invalidity Insurance Act for the Self-Employed)
WFR	*Weekblad voor Fiscaal Recht* (Dutch Tax Law Weekly)

Preface

Tax treatment of pensions is in *high* motion, not only in the Netherlands, but also across the European Union. In June 1997 the Green Paper, *Supplementary Pensions in the Single Market* was published. In this Green Paper the European Commission made an extended inventory of the tax treatment of supplementary pensions in the Member States of the European Union. In November 1997, the European Commission published a Draft Pensions Directive, especially pertinent to employees moving from one member country to another. This Directive, among other things, compelled the Foundation for European Fiscal Studies at the Erasmus University Rotterdam to organise a seminar on the tax treatment of old-age provisions in the European Union Member States on a European level, on 12 May 1998. Three experts on pensions and other old-age provisions were invited to speak and discuss this subject. The papers of those speakers are assembled in this Brochure.

The chairman of the seminar, Leo Stevens, Professor of Tax Law at the Erasmus University Rotterdam, wrote the introduction. In his chapter Humbert Drabbe, Director of Directorate D-G IV (Competition) of the European Commission in Brussels discusses pension funds in relation to European competition legislation and jurisprudence. His main conclusion is that healthy competition in the pension sector could help to ensure improved pension provisions in the future. The main question is whether the rules of competition apply to pension funds providing benefits that supplement social security systems. Given the variety of different pension systems in the Member States, it is not possible to give a single, universally accepted response. The issue must be considered on a case-by-case basis. We are awaiting developments determining whether or not exclusive rights granted to pension funds are actually justified.

Gerry Dietvorst, Professor of Retirement Provisions at Tilburg University and Director of the Fiscal and Juridical Bureau of Interpolis, outlines pension schemes in various European Union Member States in his chapter. After analysing the main similarities and differences between pension schemes, Dietvorst's conclusions, among others, are that nearly all Member States grant tax privileges encouraging individuals to make supplementary provisions. These supplementary provisions are distinguished both by the level of coverage recommended, which varies greatly and is largely determined by the extent of coverage provided by the social security systems of the different Member States, and by determining whether the primary pensions are compulsory.

The third chapter by Peter Kavelaars, Professor of Tax Law at the Erasmus University Rotterdam and the University of Leiden and Director of Research at Deloitte & Touche Tax Advisors in Rotterdam analyses the main issues respecting pensions and other old-age provisions concerning workers in cross-border situations. His main conclusion is that problems inherent in achieving greater uniformity in the assignment rules on tax, social security and pensions need not be insurmountable, particularly in light of the fact that various rules of assignment currently in operation have been shown to lack any fundamental justification. The most logical step would be to draw up a harmonised set of assignment rules for levying tax, social security premiums and pension contributions in cross-border situations. A single, uniform system is sought.

As background reading for this Brochure, we have included the Green Paper, *Supplementary Pensions in the Single Market* (June 1997) and the definitive Council Directive 98/49/EC of 29 June 1998 on safeguarding the supplementary pension rights of employed and self-employed persons moving within the Community, published after the seminar on 25 July 1998.

The editors of this Brochure hope that publishing it will stimulate a discussion on the subject of the tax treatment of pensions and pension schemes in the Member States and on the European level.

Dirk Albregtse
Manager Tax Research
Institute for Fiscal Studies
Erasmus University Rotterdam

Leo Stevens
Professor of Tax Law
Erasmus University Rotterdam

Introduction: Pensions in the European Union

Leo Stevens

Professor of Tax Law at the Erasmus University, Rotterdam and Chairman of the Board of Directors of the Foundation for European Fiscal Studies

An intensive debate is currently being held in the Netherlands on the shape of the tax system in the twenty-first century. The cabinet has presented a White Paper on the subject. This seeks to reinforce the existing tax base and lists a series of measures designed to prevent this base from being eroded by the growing mobility of capital. The tax treatment of provisions for old age is an interesting aspect of this. Any further consideration of the way in which provisions for old age are treated from a tax perspective will have to focus, therefore, on facilitating trends in society such as market forces and the desire for greater freedom of choice, in addition to removing any obstacles and unintended opportunities for abuse. There are a number of issues at stake here. For example:

1. the question of whether or not the current system of providing for one's old age offers too many tax-friendly savings opportunities;
2. the need to safeguard countries' rights to levy tax in cross-border situations; and
3. the wish to neutralise the various options available for saving for one's old age.

Against this background, and also given the desire to increase individuals' involvement in the provisions for their old age, the focus in the White Paper

Taxation in the 21st Century: An Investigation is on the idea of creating a 'fiscal retirement umbrella' for coordinating all the various ways of providing for old age. This umbrella would cover pensions, life annuities and individual forms of saving schemes. Individuals would be able to decide for themselves on a combination of collective and/or individual arrangements within set parameters. The desire to make the system more flexible could also be extended to include allowing part of any individual or supplementary pension provisions to be drawn on in the event of unemployment, for training/further education purposes or in order to finance the cost of care. Any amounts drawn down should conceivably also be able to be recredited to the scheme at a later date. The Dutch cabinet has taken the view that ensuring adequate provision for old age should in any event remain a priority.

There is still a long way to go before the final shape of the fiscal retirement umbrella is decided. It will not be easy to design a scheme capable of meeting individual requirements, which is also both sufficiently flexible to cater for financial fluctuations over a relatively long period and budgetary-neutral, as well as also being relatively simple to administer. The legislative proposal submitted to the Dutch Second Chamber of Parliament, which sets out to create a framework reflecting society's desire for a more flexible system, does not inspire confidence in this respect. Furthermore, it is very important that tax measures allowing profit-taking to be postponed should not result in an erosion of the Dutch tax base when an individual emigrates to another country. Therefore, given the idea that pensions should only be taxed on disbursement *(omkeerregel)*, the subject needs to be considered at a European level.

A basic assumption underlying the application of the taxation on disbursement rule is that income set aside or contracted for pensions and other related provisions considered necessary or desirable within a society should not be regarded as income which is freely available. Income components in the form of claims to future income should not, therefore, be regarded as taxable income. They should only be regarded as taxable when the periodic payments to which the claims relate are actually disbursed. In this respect, a pension can be regarded as a form of deferred salary to be used for pension-related purposes. This idea is reinforced by the fact that membership of a pension scheme is not generally a matter on which individual employees are allowed to decide for themselves. In the vast majority of cases, membership is compulsory. Part of an employee's salary is paid in the form of a future claim, whether or not the employee wants it that way. This reinforces the idea that the accrued claims do not or at least do not yet constitute income. So, too, do the elements of solidarity incorporated in the pension premium.

The taxation on disbursement rule implies that income may be deferred for pension-related purposes and also that it may be assigned by one taxpayer to another. Tax legislators have, however, viewed the binding nature of these income components as a reason for accepting a less strict definition of income. This is seen not only in the case of pension claims, but also in annuities, in life annuity premiums, in the amounts reserved by the self-employed for their old age and in the self-employed person's allowance–all of which are tax-deductible. The Netherlands' interpretation of income is in no way unusual in this respect.

Application of the taxation on disbursement rule does, however, have implications for the tax base in the Netherlands. If you remember that total pension commitments now amount to over NLG 1,000 bn, the magnitude of the issue at stake will be clear. Applying the taxation on disbursement rule means that the right to levy tax is transferred from the home country to the source country. This can lead to fiscally motivated pension emigration, which can result in a substantial loss of revenue for the source countries. That puts pressure on the idea of taxation based on the concept of lifetime income, which is the most acceptable approach from a fiscal point of view. In the same way that the various other fiscal schemes determine income and profit conservatively and do not, therefore, apply the realisation principle too strictly, this situation also gives rise to the need for tax to be settled upon emigration.

There are several ways to ensure that the home country retains the right to levy taxes on pensions in cross-border situations. Systems could, for example, be adapted in the ways outlined below, which are also included in the White Paper *Taxation in the 21st Century: An Investigation*:

1. A decision could be taken to adopt the German system, which stipulates that pension claims are taxable in the source country and that only the interest component of pension benefits received is taxable in the country of residence;
2. In contrast to current practice, the right to levy tax on pension benefits could be assigned wholly to the source country;
3. A decision could be taken to opt for an arbitral solution to the question of which country has the right to levy tax by giving the source country the right to levy a withholding tax on pension benefits received. This could either be offset against income tax levied in the source country on the pension benefits received or taken account of in another way in the country of residence by means of a tax reduction on the said pension benefits;
4. Another possibility would be to levy an exit tax on the value of the pension claims accrued in the source country as at the date of emigration. The White Paper *Taxation in the 21st Century: An Investigation* achieves this by making application of the taxation on disbursement rule optional.

Any levies which effectively restrict mobility would clearly be out of place in a European context, where the free movement of persons, goods, services and capital is enshrined in the EC Treaty. Levying an exit tax would contravene the spirit of the EC Treaty. Another problem would be the frequent wish of national tax authorities to attach restrictive conditions to the opportunities for making provision for one's old age, with the only purpose of these conditions being to protect the relevant national authorities' rights to levy tax on any benefits received. The most important cases from a European perspective are Case C-204/90 *Bachmann* [1992] ECR 249 (28 January 1992, ECJ), Case C-80/94 *Wielockx* [1995] (11 August 1995,

ECJ) BNB 1995/319* and the more recent Case C-118/96 *Safir* (28 April 1998, ECJ) BNB 1999/6.

For this reason, legislators in the European Union Member States will need to reassess the fiscal regulations relating to the assignment of their rights to levy taxes on pension claims. The Dutch State Secretary of Finance, Mr. Vermeend, anticipated this development in his memorandum entitled *Uitgangspunten van het beleid op het terrein van het internationaal fiscaal (verdrags)recht* (Starting points (Principles) of international tax (treaty)policy). Fiscal regulations are also relevant, however, to those involved in administering pensions. In the Netherlands, the reason for requiring pension administrators to fulfil certain conditions is not primarily because of a wish to protect the country's right to levy tax, but is more related to the desire to prevent pension arrangements being misused. Administrators have to operate in an area in which the Dutch tax authorities have jurisdiction in order that sanctions can be applied in the event of powers being abused. For that reason, pension administrators in the Netherlands operate subject to very strict licensing requirements.

The *Safir* case certainly suggests that national taxation authorities should not overestimate their powers in this respect and would be well-advised to develop robust pension systems capable of meeting the European requirement for equal competitive opportunities. The need to be aware of this is becoming increasingly important, given the expectation that pension systems will in future allow more scope for flexibility. The European Fiscal Studies Foundation is seeking to contribute to this discussion by organising the conference on pensions in a European context.

Pension Funds and Competition

Humbert Drabbe

Director Directorate D-G IV of the European Commission, Brussels

1 Introduction

The Green Paper *Supplementary Pensions in the Single Market,* published in June 1997, addresses three topics:

- how can an enhanced role for pension funds meet the growing need for supplementary pension financing beyond the first pillar?
- how can employee freedom of movement be encouraged (particularly for employees of multinational companies)?
- what are the fiscal obstacles and what can be done about them?[1]

This paper examines a subject which is not addressed in the Green Paper, i.e. the subject of pension funds and competition policy.

Consideration was given to including a section on this subject in the Green Paper. The Commission decided, however, not to do this since at the time the Court of Justice of the EC in Luxembourg was deliberating on whether or not pension funds were actually covered by competition law (the *Brentjes* case, C-115, C-116 and C-117/97, and *Drijvende Bokken* case, C-219/91). We

[1] For the text of the Green Paper see Appendix A.

have since progressed from there and a plausible, provisional line of reasoning can now be developed.

There are two reasons why this issue is important:

1. Pension funds have often been granted exclusive rights to a fixed group of clients by the relevant authorities. These rights determine, therefore, their position *viz-à-viz* potential competitors such as life assurance companies, which are also able to provide pension facilities.
2. The exclusive rights mean that employees or professional practitioners are obliged to join a specific pension fund and do not, therefore, have the right to opt for pension provisions of their own choice.

The latter subject in particular has been and remains an issue on which the Court has been deliberating, and I shall attempt to bring some structure into the discussion by examining legal precedents to date.

First a short outline of the most relevant aspects of the law in this context.

2 European Competition Law

The application of competition law is directly based on certain provisions of Articles 85-94 of the Treaty. For the purposes of our subject, the most important of these are Articles 85, 86 and 90.

2.1 ARTICLE 85

Article 85 covers agreements between or concerted practices by undertakings which may restrict trade within the common market.

First of all, it is the agreements between or concerted practices of *undertakings* which are of importance. In the *Höfner case,* C-244/94 the ECJ held that an undertaking could be defined as any entity engaged in commercial activity, irrespective of its legal form and the way in which it was financed. What is important, therefore, is to establish whether or not the activity in which the entity is engaged is of a commercial nature. Let me give you a few examples. An association of undertakings may in itself constitute an undertaking. So, too, may a self-employed individual such as a professional practitioner, or artists selling their work on a commercial basis. Whether or not the undertaking has a profit motive is not of relevance.

Secondly, Article 85 covers *agreements and concerted practices* involving at least two parties, in contrast to Article 86 which deals with the practices of a single party.

Thirdly, Article 85 deals with arrangements which *restrict* competition, i.e. arrangements which have as their object or result in the restriction or distortion of competition within the common market. What is meant is not every single restriction agreed upon between undertakings–say, for example, a straightforward contract. No, what is meant are those arrangements which have the object or effect of undermining the competitive market structure in a *noticeable way*. Whether or not an action is 'noticeable' largely depends on the parties' positions in the relevant market. Restrictive practices will be more noticeable in the event of an undertaking having a dominant market share than if it is only a small player in the market.

For Article 85 to apply, the agreements or practices must also be capable of adversely affecting *trade between Member States*. Simply having the potential to affect trade adversely is sufficient. What has to be decided is whether a specific situation is a matter for Brussels or for the anti-trust authorities in the relevant Member State.

The list of prohibitions is not exhaustive: price fixing and agreements to share markets are mortal sins, but any other forms of agreement or concerted practices which can be defined are also prohibited under Article 85(2). This means that they are prohibited with direct effect, unless they are exempt under Article 85(3), which makes provision for the possibility of exemptions for certain agreements or practices. These exemptions should on the one hand serve the cause of economic progress, whilst allowing consumers to share fairly in the benefits of such arrangements, and on the other hand be indispensable if the specific positive effect is to be achieved, whilst not eliminating competition completely in the relevant market.

Under the terms of Article 85(3), therefore, an analysis is needed of the advantages and disadvantages of any agreements between undertakings which restrict or distort competition.

It is also clear that the decision whether or not to apply these general principles needs to be taken on a case-by-case basis. In comparable cases the principles should of course be applied to the same extent, which is why previous decisions by the Commission and by the ECJ in individual cases are so important. The definition of an undertaking is particularly important in the arguments I will be using below since Articles 85, 86 and 90 will only apply in the event of a pension fund being regarded as an undertaking within the meaning of the Treaty.

2.2 ARTICLE 86

Article 86 prohibits an undertaking from abusing the dominant position it may have in a specific market. In contrast to Article 85, Article 86 makes no provision for exemptions. Abuse of a dominant position in a market is, therefore, always prohibited.

I should emphasise that undertakings are not prohibited from having a dominant position, but merely from abusing it. Here, too, the EC Treaty gives a number of examples; again, the list is not exhaustive. Should the Commission have grounds for suspecting abuse, it first has to demonstrate that there is a dominant position and then that this is being abused.

2.3 ARTICLE 90

Articles 85 and 86 are concerned specifically with undertakings, whilst Article 90 also covers the public sector ('public undertakings'). Article 90(1) states that in the case of public undertakings and undertakings to which Member States have granted exclusive rights or a monopoly, Member States shall neither enact nor maintain in force any measures contrary to the rules contained in the Treaty, specifically the rules relating to competition policy.

Article 90(2) relates to undertakings entrusted with the operation of services of general economic interest. It states that the rules of competition will apply in so far as the application of such rules does not obstruct the performance of the particular task entrusted to the undertakings. Given the reference to the competition rules, it follows that Article 90 applies in conjunction with other rules of competition such as Articles 85 and 86.

The telecom sector is an example of a group of undertakings to which Member States have granted certain exclusive rights under Article 90(1). The Member States are not allowed to enact or maintain in force any measures which would leave an undertaking no option but to act contrary to Article 86 (abuse of a dominant position).

Article 90(2) allows for undertakings to be exempt in principle from application of the rules of competition in the event that they have been entrusted with the operation of public services by a public body and that the restricting of competition is essential for the operation of these particular services.

3 Pension Funds and Competition

You will be aware of the concept of dividing the pensions sector into three columns or pillars. Perhaps it would be clearer to refer to three complementary layers. The first layer is the basic pension provisions; in other words, the social security system, which varies in size from country to country. The size of the second layer is proportionately larger or smaller. For that reason, the extent to which competition legislation applies also varies considerably from country to country as the first layer, the social security system, will in any event be outside the scope of the legislation.

The second layer is the pension provisions made by undertakings for their employees. In the Netherlands, pension funds have been set up on a sector basis, including those pension funds for specific professions such as physiotherapists and company pension funds. The third layer comprises the pension provisions made by private individuals to supplement the first two layers. This layer has traditionally been provided by life assurance companies, but the market is now actually far larger and involves a multitude of savings and investment products providers competing with the traditional life assurance companies. The rules of competition will apply in any event to this market.

The question of whether or not competition law should in principle apply relates specifically, therefore, to the second layer; in other words, to supplementary, employment-related pension provisions. Clearly, the more similar the structure of the second layer is to the social security system, the more difficult it is to answer the question. In France, for example, supplementary, employment-related pensions are financed on an apportionment basis ('pay as you go'), which is a typical feature of social security systems. The degree of solidarity in the various systems also varies considerably from country to country. In principle, the French supplementary system covers the whole working population and is in that respect very similar to the various social security systems in operation. In contrast, employee pension funds in the Netherlands provide cover to a clearly defined, relatively limited group of employees. The question is, therefore, whether there are clear criteria which can be used to decide whether an undertaking providing employee pensions to supplement the provisions of the social security system is actually subject to the rules of competition.

You will have noticed that the Articles relating to competition only apply in the case of an undertaking; in other words, in the event of a pension fund being engaged in a commercial activity.

The ECJ has taken two decisions of particular relevance in this context: its decisions in the *Poucet & Pistre* case, C-155/91 and C-160/91 in 1993 and the *FFSA v. French Ministry of Agriculture* case, C-244/94 in 1995.

4 Court of Justice Decisions

In 1993 the ECJ decided in the *Poucet & Pistre* case that two French pension funds, which had been appointed by the French authorities as the only providers of basic healthcare insurance and pensions, were not engaged in commercial activity and were, therefore, not subject to the rules of competition. Poucet and Pistre were two employees who, whilst not objecting to the legal obligation to be insured, maintained that they should be free to arrange healthcare insurance for themselves with a commercial insurer.

As mentioned above, the ECJ had previously ruled in the *Höfner* case that the term 'undertaking' should be interpreted as meaning any entity engaged in commercial activity, irrespective of its legal form and the way in which it was financed. In the *Poucet & Pistre* case the ECJ ruled that this interpretation excluded entities entrusted with operating compulsory social security schemes based on the principle of solidarity. The ECJ based its decision on the considerable degree of solidarity in the relevant insurance system and concluded that in this case there was no engagement in commercial activity. It singled out the following aspects as being of particular relevance:

- in this specific sickness and maternity insurance scheme all claimants received the same benefits, whilst contributions were related proportionately to income;

- the scheme's old-age pensions were financed on a 'pay as you go' basis by contributions made by current employees. Moreover, the pension entitlements defined in law were not proportionate to the contributions paid;
- lastly, those schemes with a surplus contributed to the financing of schemes with financial problems of a structural nature.

In view of this solidarity element, the various schemes had to be operated by a single party and joining one of the schemes needed to be compulsory. The ECJ's decision was clearly based, therefore, on the degree of solidarity in the specific insurance system.

I do not have any problem with this decision as such, i.e. with the fact that the competition rules were deemed not to be applicable. The question, however, is whether the ECJ actually applied the right criterion when coming to its decision.

Two years after its decision in the *Poucet & Pistre* case, the ECJ was asked to decide on the question of whether a French pension fund providing pensions for employees in the agricultural sector to supplement their basic state pensions should be regarded as an undertaking within the meaning of the competition rules. This was the *FFSA v. French Ministry of Agriculture* case. Membership of this particular funded pension scheme was optional. The benefits to which employees were entitled depended solely on the amount of their contributions and the results of the investments made by the fund's management. In this case, the ECJ decided that the fund was engaged in commercial activity and was in competition with life assurance companies. A farmer or other agricultural employee wanting to supplement a basic pension would choose whichever provider was able to guarantee the best investment results when deciding between the above fund or a life assurance company. Here, therefore, it is a case of second-pillar provisions.

After deciding that the entity should thus be regarded as an undertaking, the ECJ stated that the fact that the scheme in question contained elements of solidarity had no bearing on this definition. According to the ECJ, the solidarity principle was reflected in the fact that:

- contributions were not determined by risk;
- in the event of a member's premature death, the assets corresponding to the contributions paid would be released to the scheme;
- in the event of illness, individuals were exempt from contributing and, lastly,
- payment of contributions could be suspended temporarily for reasons relating to a company's economic situation.

Similar sorts of arrangements are also, however, included or can be included in collective life assurance schemes. Furthermore, the ECJ considered that, given the optional nature of the scheme, the solidarity principle was in any event of very limited significance and did not, therefore, detract from the commercial nature of the activity in which the fund's management was engaged.

What could still be examined, according to the ECJ, was whether the solidarity argument could be used to justify the exclusive right granted to the entity to provide an old age pension insurance scheme, with tax-deductible contributions; in other words, whether the exclusive right granted could be justified under Article 90(2) of the EC Treaty. The ECJ did not, however, address that issue in any further detail.

An interesting aspect is that the French commercial insurers have in fact brought the issue of the legality of the fund's monopoly before the French Council of State. And what is more, the Council of State found in their favour. It ruled that the monopoly did indeed constitute an abuse of a dominant position under Article 86 of the EC Treaty.

The decision in the *FFSA* case has effectively refined the definition of solidarity. The question, however, is–as I mentioned earlier–whether the degree of solidarity should actually be the criterion for determining whether or not there is commercial activity and whether or not, therefore, the pension fund is an undertaking. Solidarity is a difficult concept to define. There are also, of course, varying degrees of solidarity. Where should the boundary be drawn? When does solidarity mean that an entity is an undertaking and when does it not?

In my view, it would be better to apply two clear criteria to determine whether an entity should be regarded as an undertaking:

1. whether or not it is free to determine the price of the product, and
2. whether or not it is free to define the product, if necessary within a general legal framework.

The pension fund in the *Poucet & Pistre* case had absolutely no say in deciding the level of premiums needing to be paid by members. Nor had it any input in the contents of the insurance product. It had, therefore, no independent decision-making powers in respect of the two main features of its product: price and quality. My view is that funds lacking such decision-making powers are not engaged in commercial activity as price and quality are precisely the elements used by businesses as a basis for competing with one another. The pension provisions in the *Poucet & Pistre* case were clearly first-pillar provisions. In contrast, the second French case involved second-pillar provisions, where the fund was free to decide on both the price and quality of its product.

5 Cases Involving Dutch Pension Funds

Interestingly enough, there are two cases (preliminary references) involving Dutch pension funds which are currently before the ECJ. These are the *Brentjes v. Stichting Pensioenfonds voor de handel in bouwmaterialen* case and the *Maatschappij Drijvende Bokken v. Stichting Pensioenfonds voor de vervoer-en havenbedrijven* case. The questions arising in these cases have been put by Dutch judges, including those at the Supreme Court of the Netherlands. The issue in these cases is not only the question of whether the pension funds should be regarded as undertakings and, therefore, as being engaged in commercial activity, but also whether the exclusive rights granted to the funds in law are actually justified. As I indicated earlier, the ECJ did touch on this problem briefly in its decision in the *FFSA* case. In the Dutch cases, both pension funds have a monopoly because all insurable employees in the sector are obliged by law to join the sector's pension fund. You may be aware that under the Company Pension Fund (Obligatory Participation) Act, the Minister of Social Affairs is authorised, at the request of a sector's management and employee representatives, to declare membership of the company pension fund to be compulsory for all or certain groups of employees in the sector or specific company. This was what had actually happened in both pension fund cases.

Under Dutch law, all insurable employees are required to join the pension fund, and the pension fund is not allowed to select participants on the basis of age, sex or health. The degree of solidarity is, therefore, no different from that in the *Poucet & Pistre* case, which was the first case I mentioned. In other respects, however, the Dutch pension funds do differ from the fund in the *Poucet & Pistre* case since they are able to determine the level of contributions and the contents of their products themselves. Both Dutch pension funds are funded schemes: they invest the contributions and use the proceeds to finance pensions. In contrast, the pension funds in the *Poucet & Pistre* case operated on a 'pay as you go' basis: contributions paid by current employees were immediately paid out as pensions to current pensioners. The Dutch pension funds are, therefore, more similar to the pension fund in the *FFSA* case, and both are in the second pillar.

In the written comments on the Dutch cases submitted by the Commission to the ECJ, the Commission took the view that the Dutch pension funds were engaged in commercial activity. The decisive factor for the Commission was whether a pension fund had independent decision-making powers in respect of the two most important elements of its activity, that is price (the contributions) and content of the product (the pensions).

It should be noted that one difference with the *FFSA* case is that joining either of the Dutch pension funds was compulsory. This means that there is a high degree of solidarity. This difference relates only to the legal basis of the funds' activities. As I mentioned, it should not be forgotten that the undertakings in a specific sector are allowed by law to decide whether or not to opt for a supplementary pension scheme. Moreover, if the undertakings should so wish, they are also entitled to arrange for pension provisions to be made at either a company or sector level. The undertakings are even allowed to contract management of the pension fund to a private insurance company. The state only becomes involved if management and employees want it to. This form of intervention does not change the nature of the activities in question in any way.

The fact that the pension funds capitalise the contributions is not a decisive factor. The ECJ has stated on several occasions that the method of financing a certain activity is irrelevant when determining whether an activity is of a commercial nature or not.

The Commission acknowledges that all employees pay the same percentage of their salary in pension contributions. In other words, individual contributions do not reflect the cost of the risks represented by individual participants. The Commission's view is that this feature does not detract from the commercial nature of the fund's activity. What is important is that the fund has to keep revenues and costs in equilibrium, which is a restriction that the fund has in common with commercial insurers. The supervisory authorities will also ensure that these pension funds–just like commercial insurers–remain financially healthy.

6 Exclusive Rights of Pension Funds

As you will be able to conclude from the above, the Commission views the degree of solidarity–and here I am referring to the *Poucet & Pistre* case–as irrelevant to the question of whether or not the Dutch pension funds are engaged in a commercial activity. The degree of solidarity is, however, very important when deciding whether the exclusive rights granted to these funds are actually justified, that is whether or not they are covered by the exemptions provided for under Article 90(2) of the EC Treaty.

The funds have been granted exclusive rights because employees currently active in the relevant sector are obliged to become members. The state has, therefore, provided the funds with a captive client base. The funds do not have to compete with other funds and are regarded as undertakings to which a Member State has granted exclusive rights within the meaning of Article 90(1) of the EC Treaty. If it can be argued that these pension funds have been entrusted with the operation of services of general economic interest under the meaning of Article 90(2), the rules of competition will in principle not be applicable.

These pension funds may indeed be able to be regarded as undertakings entrusted with the operation of services of general economic interest. The fact that joining them is compulsory could be viewed as a necessary means of ensuring that the pensions provided in a specific sector contain a sufficient element of solidarity. Otherwise, the possibility of 'good risks' being accepted and 'bad risks' being rejected could not be ruled out. There are, however, arguments against exempting these pension funds from the competition rules. The question arises as to whether the funds have actually been *entrusted* with management within the meaning of the case law of the ECJ. The fact that membership is compulsory is actually because management and employee representatives in the sector wanted it to be so. The ECJ would seem, however, to prefer a stricter interpretation.

Secondly, the fact that they have been granted exclusive legal rights must be because these rights are deemed to be necessary in order to ensure proper management of the pension arrangements. Obviously, the need for these rights has to be determined on a case-by-case basis. The fact that pension funds in certain sectors function well without employees being obliged to join (i.e. where management and employee representatives have not requested the Minister of Social Affairs to make membership compulsory) indicates that these legal monopolies are not automatically indispensable.

Another argument pointing in favour of allowing these exclusive rights to continue is that the ECJ allows Member States considerable freedom to structure their own social security systems as they want, in consultation with management and employee representatives. Since we are talking about *supplementary* pension provisions, I think it is quite likely that the ECJ will allow parties considerable scope to decide on the exact contents of these provisions.

7 Conclusion

Healthy competition in the pension sector could help to ensure good pension provisions in the future. The crucial issue that I have examined is whether the rules of competition apply to pension funds providing benefits which supplement the social security systems. In other words, can a pension fund constitute an undertaking? Given the variety of different pension systems in the Member States, it is not possible to give a single, generally applicable answer. The issue has to be looked at on a case-by-case basis. The ECJ's decisions have been based in principle on the degree of solidarity present, which is also a factor that is difficult to define and which maybe ought not to be the decisive criterion. In the two Dutch cases, the ECJ may take up the Commission's suggestion of using another criterion, i.e. the extent to which a pension fund is free to determine the price and content of its product. We are awaiting developments, therefore, on both this subject and the applicability of Article 90 to the issue of whether or not exclusive rights granted to pension funds are actually justified.

Pensions: Uniform or Coordinated[1]

Gerry Dietvorst

Professor of Retirement Provisions at the Tilburg University and Director of Fiscal and Juridicial Bureau Interpolis

1 Introduction

The main focus of this paper is on the pension arrangements in various European countries.

As in many other situations, the saying 'each to his own' also applies in the case of pensions. What the various forms of retirement provisions in the European Union have in common is that they can all be divided into a three-pillar structure. Usually, however, the contents of these structures differ significantly from country to country. The tax-deductible pension allowance for the self-employed in the Netherlands is, for example, totally unknown in other European countries. As, too, is the idea of a managing director/ majority shareholder of a company managing his own pension or setting up a private company specifically for this purpose. Neither will it be any surprise to hear that the system of tax-deductible annuity premiums in the Netherlands is also a completely unknown phenomenon in other Member States.

An example of pension differences close to home is Belgium, where pensions are commutable. Indeed, from a fiscal perspective it is actually

[1] The information on specific countries provided here is partly based on research I did as a member of the committee set up by the Association of Fiscal Science.

preferable to commute the pension rather than to receive the benefits on a recurrent basis. For that reason, pensions are normally commuted on retirement. Another example is the United Kingdom, where partial commutation is allowed on an individual's retirement date. In contrast, the Dutch Pension and Savings Funds Act actually prohibits pension commutation. Even after a value transfer abroad in the case of employees emigrating and accepting a job in another country, pensions are not permitted to be commuted. Opinions differ on whether the Dutch Pension and Savings Funds Act would actually be able to be enforced abroad. Obviously, the tax treatment in the Netherlands of life assurance policies and the benefits paid out under them is not the only way. What the Netherlands regards as an endowment insurance from a tax perspective could well be regarded simply as a bank account in another European Union country. The fact the countries have sovereignty in respect of direct taxation means that there is unlikely to be any significant change in this situation in the near future. I see no prospect of a single European system for retirement provisions within the next 10 years. My view is that there are more likely to be opportunities for coordinating rules and systems, rather than there being a trend towards uniformity.

This paper is structured as follows: first, it briefly outlines the three-pillar structure in the Netherlands. There follows a short description of the current situation in specific countries. It then goes on to focus on occupational pension schemes. In most Member States, the latter work on the basis of tax deferment and are only taxed upon disbursement (*omkeerregel*). The specific provisions of such pension schemes and the tax rules applying to them vary greatly from country to country.

2 Three-Pillar Structure

The idea of a three-pillar structure is commonly used in the case of retirement provisions, particularly in an international context. The fiscal and legal rules, as well as the regulations governing fund administrators and those entitled to operate in the market, are different in each pillar. There are also substantial differences between the methods of financing the various pillars and between the various countries.

Chart 1 Three pillars in the Netherlands

RETIREMENT PROVISIONS

State old-age pension	Occupational pension - BPF/Insurance companies - Company pension fund	Capital sum insurance
Surviving dependants pension	Occupational pension fund	Annuity insurance
Invalidity pension	Pension allowance for self-employed. Discontinuity profit used for purchase of annuity.	

- The essence of the first pillar is that it is intended to comprise a basic provision and cover a wide range of individuals. For the sake of convenience, this pillar is referred to as the state old-age pension.
- The provisions and rules in the second pillar are directly linked to the performance of work. They apply to pensions provided by employers to employees, as well as to retirement pensions arranged by the self-employed for themselves and to pensions designed to cover the cost of caring for dependants in the event of an employee or former employee's death or invalidity.
- The third pillar relates to supplementary, voluntary provisions such as capital sum and annuity insurance, where there is no direct relationship to the performance of work. These types of insurance have in common the fact that they are voluntary and up to individual citizens to arrange. The nature of these types of arrangement means that they are always financed on a funded basis. For this reason, only the tax treatment of these provisions will be discussed here.
- The importance of the various pillars varies from country to country. The more extensive the coverage provided by the first pillar, the less important the second and third pillars will be. Similarly, if occupational pensions provide extensive coverage, the first and third pillars will be of less importance.

3 *Taxation in the 21st Century: An Investigation*

In late 1997 the Dutch Ministry of Finance presented a White Paper entitled *Taxation in the 21st Century: An Investigation.* In it, the plans for the structure of the Dutch pensions system in the twenty-first century were outlined.

The basic concept on which this White Paper is based is simple and straightforward: the tax system can be used to help all taxpayers to make adequate provision for their old age, and that is all that can be expected of it. Both the extent and duration of the tax measures designed for this purpose are restricted; for example, countries look for ways to realise or safeguard their fiscal claims on accrued pension provisions at the time of or subsequent to an individual's emigration. In many cases, choices have to be made. Nevertheless, this fundamental concept will form the basis for further discussion and ideas on the subject.

The White Paper states the following in respect of retirement provisions:[2]

1. the tax regime applying to pensions and annuities in the Netherlands is generous in comparison with most other countries, with the annual tax-deductible allowance for retirement provisions being one of the highest anywhere;
2. the current system of taxation often results in a lower tariff being applied to pensions when they are paid out than whilst they are being built up;
3. the current system does not reflect the growing mobility of individuals;
4. this can result in tax on pension and annuity benefits increasingly being paid in countries other than the Netherlands;
5. this development leads to an erosion of the Netherlands' tax base and to a loss of tax revenues;
6. extensive use is made of the facilities available for making provision for old age. In the event of the tax system being revised, the question of whether the scope of the various facilities is still in line with society's views on the issue will have to be considered.

The White Paper comes out clearly in favour of retaining the fiscal privileges designed to assist the process of providing for old age. It makes the implicit assumption that abolition of the taxation on disbursement rule (*omkeerregel*) would have implications for the annuities regime and the tax-deductible pension allowance for the self-employed.[3]

The general view would seem to be in favour of retaining the taxation on disbursement rule–despite the direct increase of around NLG 15 bn in government revenues if it were to be abolished and the various different forms of savings were to be neutralised from a tax perspective. Although

---

[2] See ch. 5.0, p. 46.
[3] See p. 48.

abolishing the taxation on disbursement rule would certainly help to simplify taxation legislation, taxing pension claims would not reflect individuals' understanding of income. Moreover, the Netherlands would then be more or less the only country in the European Union where the fiscal measures designed to assist individuals to make adequate retirement provisions did not work on the basis of tax deferment. Abolition of this principle would result in a number of complications in international situations; for example, if a pension built up in the Netherlands were paid out abroad, the pension claim already would have been taxed in the Netherlands and the benefits would then be taxed again in the country of residence.

After publication of the taxation plan for the twenty-first century, Van Wijnbergen[4] again attacked the principle of the taxation on disbursement rule, calling it the largest subsidy in the Dutch tax system. What he was referring to was the fact that most social security premiums are no longer payable once an individual reaches the age of 65. Consequently, tax is deferred at a much higher rate than is ultimately levied on the benefits disbursed. Van Wijnbergen's analysis is certainly correct, but that is not sufficient reason in itself to abolish the taxation on disbursement rule. What he objects to is the system used for levying social security premiums. Financing social security from general government revenues, as the White Paper proposes, would mean an end to subsidies.

In early 1997, the Netherlands Federation of Tax Advisors, backed up by Giele, also came out in favour of this.[5] My arguments for retaining the taxation on disbursement rule were seemingly not enough to convince Van Wijnbergen.[6] I will briefly list the various arguments used in defence of the taxation on disbursement rule:

1. the idea of deferring income is an inherent part of retirement provisions: income which has to be set aside to ensure adequate provision for one's old age is not part of individuals' current taxable and disposable income;
2. there are budgetary benefits for the government in the short term, but in the long term the government would be biting the hand that feeds it;
3. the taxation on disbursement rule reflects individuals' understanding of income; paying tax on something that you have not received and will maybe never receive is not an attractive proposition for anyone;
4. it will be impossible to find an acceptable way of valuing and taxing claims, not least because in many cases there will be no direct relationship between the premiums paid and the claims;

---

4 S.G.J. Van Wijnbergen, Secretary-General of the Ministry of Economic Affairs, 'Nederland weer aan het werk' *Economisch-Statistische Berichten* 7 November 1998.

5 *Netherlands Government Gazette* 13 May 1997.

6 See 'Fiscale behandeling pensioenen en lijfrenten anders aanpakken?' *Netherlands Government Gazette* 21 May 1997.

5. the problems involved in the transition phase (a very long period) will cause such disruption that a fundamental change in the current fiscal treatment of pension arrangements will not be feasible;
6. the international dimension will create an added complication: the Netherlands would become an attractive country for immigrants over the age of 65 if pension benefits were not taxed.[7] In addition, it would be impossible to emigrate from the Netherlands because pension benefits which had already been taxed at the claims stage in the Netherlands would then be taxed again in the new country of residence.[8]

4 Umbrella Approach[9]

A comprehensive definition of pensions is being considered. The idea of an overall retirement umbrella has, for example, been conceived as a means of increasing individuals' awareness of their provisions for old age. This retirement umbrella would encompass a comprehensive range of tax facilities designed to help individuals to provide for their old age via:

- collective pension schemes;
- annuity insurance;
- fiscal pension allowance for the self-employed;
- retirement or investment accounts subject to special conditions

5 Green Paper: *Supplementary Pensions in the Single Market*

The Green Paper provides a good overview of the specific features of each of the three pillars of pension provisions in the European Union, as well as emphasising their importance (in terms of the extent of cover provided) *viz-à-viz* total pension benefits. The importance of the different pillars varies significantly from country to country. The average percentage of total pension benefits represented by each of the separate pillars in the various countries is as follows:

- First pillar: state pension schemes (compulsory membership) and related in part to years of service and income: 88.8 per cent;

---

[7] I must admit that one positive effect would be that tax exiles would perhaps be more likely to return to the Netherlands, not only because of its better retirement and health care provisions, but also for tax reasons.

[8] I realise that this problem could be resolved via double taxation treaties or a European Union Regulation.

[9] See pp. 47, 51.

- Second pillar: occupational pension schemes: 7 per cent;[10]
- Third pillar: private life assurance policies (largely pension savings schemes): 0.9 per cent.[11]

These figures show that occupational pensions represent a relatively small share of total pensions in the European Union.

The problem facing all Western countries, specifically in respect of their state pension schemes, is that of an ageing population. Ways of dealing with the effect of the baby boom are being considered in a number of countries, some of which have introduced changes to their pension systems in recent years. The measures that have been implemented vary considerably, with some countries choosing to increase premiums and/or reduce benefits and others choosing to raise the pensionable age. In certain countries, for example Finland, where benefit levels are influenced by other pension income, people are optimistic about the result of efforts to deal with the issue of the ageing population.

The stance taken in the Green Paper on the tax treatment of retirement provisions is that pensions are essentially an issue for the Member States themselves to decide on and that the fiscal rules and regulations are matters which evolve over a period of years. The diversity of the various systems in operation means that a pension scheme may qualify in one country, but not in another. The European Commission believes that the system of assigning pension benefits, for tax purposes, to the country of residence works well.

It is striking that only a few Member States allow migrants to deduct from tax any pension premiums paid into a 'tax-approved scheme' in another country. The Commission believes that mutual recognition of pension arrangements will remove the obstacles standing in the way of labour mobility.

Any subsequent references to tax should be understood as referring to income or wage taxes as capital and inheritance taxes will not be discussed.

6 Dilemmas and Solutions: A Uniform Framework, Mutual Recognition or Abolition of the Taxation on Disbursement Rule?

One of the most important features in an international context is the fact that pensions involve the payment of tax being deferred. The country paying or assigning the pensions will not want to lose its tax claim on the pensions paid or transfer values assigned. Currently, almost all treaties stipulate that pension benefits disbursed (including any commuted payments) should be taxed in the country of residence.

---

10 In the Netherlands, second-pillar pensions represent almost one-third of total pension benefits.

11 Other benefits relate, for example, to welfare benefit.

Would there be more acceptable legislation from the perspective of retaining rights to the claim and from a regulatory point of view if there were to be a uniform pensions framework or mutual recognition of pension schemes or if the taxation on disbursement rule were to be abolished?

Mutual recognition of pension arrangements would represent a step forward in terms of the free movement of persons, particularly in the case of frontier workers and certainly if this were to be combined with agreements on a uniform framework for pensions. This would include tax ceilings, making benefits flexible, providing opportunities for commutation and the definition of eligible individuals. The main obstacle would not seem to me to be the idea of a tax ceiling, but rather the question of whether pensions should be able to be commuted and, if so, to what extent. Cultural differences in the pensions sphere are a very important element in this respect.

The subject of frontier workers demands particular attention since it involves income from labour being assigned to the host country for tax purposes, whilst individuals have no or, at least, no significant other income in that country and nor do they have any pension arrangements there. If the country in which an individual works does not allow annuity premiums paid by the individual to be deducted from tax, the individual is unable to make use of the fiscal privileges available for building up a retirement provision since there is no income against which the annuity premiums can be offset. The solution to this problem would be to allow annuity premiums to be deducted in the country in which the individual is working. I believe incidentally that, given the ECJ's decision in the *Schumacker* case on 14 January 1995 (C-279/93 *Finanzamt Köln-Altstadt v. Schumacker*) BNB 1995/107, the host country—in the case of, say, the Netherlands and Germany—would have to allow annuity premiums to be deducted from tax.

Although I am very much in favour of fiscal assistance being provided in the form of the taxation on disbursement rule and deductible annuity premiums in order to encourage the building up of retirement provisions, I would consider it worthwhile examining the issue of abolishing the various fiscal privileges in their current form, particularly given the growing internationalisation of retirement provisions. The issues of the transfer value, retention of the tax claim and the requirement for the administrator to be resident would then be seen in a different light and would be much easier to resolve.

There are two ways of abolishing the fiscal privileges: firstly, taxing the claim and allowing the benefit to be paid out completely free of tax. Another method, albeit a method which would contravene the normal understanding of income, would be to tax the claim at an attractive rate and to allow the benefits to be paid out in due course either fully or partially free of tax. The interest component of the benefit would then be taxed. Tax bands or percentages could also be agreed at a European Union level. The problem of retaining the right to tax the accrued claim would then be limited to the capital growth.

The arrangements for the transition period would present a specific problem. By definition, the periods involved would be long or very long. A 25-year-old who has contributed for one year to a pension operating on a deferred tax basis will be reminded of the previous regime for a further 50-60 years.

The only solution in this respect is rigorous intervention: pay the tax on current pension claims and reserves in one go. The Netherlands Federation of Tax Advisors put forward a proposal along these lines in 1997. Such a solution would have budgetary benefits for the government in the short term as the extra revenues generated could be used to reduce state debt. It also has the advantage of simplicity: no sanctions if you no longer meet the conditions for a pension or annuity! Retaining the right to tax the claim would then acquire a different dimension.

7 Pension Systems in Various European Countries

This section provides an overview of a number of features of retirement provisions in various European countries. In certain cases, the terminology used in specific countries has not been translated since this would detract too much from the specific nature of the provisions and their purpose.

7.1 Austria

7.1.1 First pillar

The state pension is a basic provision and is financed on a pay-as-you-go (PAYG) basis. It covers employees, apprentices, trainees and the self-employed. Benefits are related to earnings during an individual's working life and the insured period. The maximum amount payable is 79.5 per cent of pensionable salary: 1.9 per cent for each of the first 30 insured years and 1.5 per cent for each of the following 15 years. Pensionable salary is calculated on the basis of an individual's highest salary in a 15-year period.

The premium is paid by employers (12.55 per cent of salaries) and employees (10.25 per cent). The pensionable age is 65 for men and 60 for women. The female retirement age is gradually being raised to 65 (between 2024 and 2033). Early retirement is possible, without a reduction in benefits, providing an individual has been insured for at least 35 years. Deferment will result in a higher pension. Partial early retirement is also possible.

7.1.2 Second pillar

Pensions are neither compulsory for the population as a whole nor in specific sectors. The taxation on disbursement rule is applied. Second-pillar pensions do not represent a substantial share of overall pension provisions in Austria. First-pillar provisions represent 93 per cent of total benefits, with only 4 per cent of benefits relating to second-pillar provisions. The degree of cover is, therefore, very limited. The content of the supplementary, funded pension schemes varies from scheme to scheme. It is impossible to give a general overview, both in terms of premiums and in terms of the cover provided. The pensionable age is the same as in the first pillar: 65 for men and 60 for women. The second-pillar provisions take no account of the state pension scheme.

The taxation on disbursement rule applies unless premiums are in excess of ATS 4,000. The Austrian system operates in a similar way to the German system, with a distinction being drawn between *Direktzusagen*[12] (62 per cent), *Pensionskassen* (21 per cent) and life insurance companies (17 per cent).

7.1.3 *Third pillar*

Similarly, the third pillar is not extensive in Austria. Only 3 per cent of pension benefits relate to third-pillar provisions. This is because of the ending in 1988 of the tax measures which encouraged individuals to make retirement provisions for themselves. The general rule is that only 50 per cent of any life assurance premiums (both capital sum and annuity policies) are deductible from taxable earnings as an exceptional expense (1994: a maximum of 50 per cent of ATS 40,000 per person). In the case of annuities, the policy must be a life annuity. Capital sum policies are required to be for a term of 20 years.

7.2 BELGIUM

7.2.1 *First pillar*

The state pension is financed by the apportionment method (PAYG). Benefits are related to income earned during an individual's active working life. The scheme covers employees, civil servants and the self-employed. Different rules apply to each of these separate groups. Non-management employees receive an average of 70 per cent (net) of their earnings prior to retirement, whilst managers receive 45 per cent and senior managers 32 per cent.

First-pillar benefits paid to civil servants are substantially higher than those paid to employees and the self-employed: the civil service pension is based on an individual's income in the five years prior to retirement instead of on the average income during the insured period, which is how others covered by the state scheme are paid. Civil service pensions are financed by the state on a fully funded basis.

Premiums are as follows: the employer pays 8.86 per cent of the salary, the employee 7.5 per cent and the state 2.5 per cent. There is no maximum cut-off for premiums.

The official pensionable age is flexible. Both men and women can choose to retire at any age between 60 and 65. Deferring retirement results in higher benefits.

---

[12] The employer makes a commitment to pay a pension and remains responsible for managing this commitment.

7.2.2 *Second pillar*

Pensions are not compulsory. Voluntary pension schemes, which cover 31 per cent of employees, are partly financed on a PAYG basis and partly on a funded basis. Belgium applies the taxation on disbursement rule to pensions. Benefits paid out under these schemes represent 8 per cent of total pensions. The pension fund administrator has to be based in Belgium. The objective of these pension schemes is generally to provide 60 per cent of final salary (including the state pension). The taxation on disbursement rule is restricted to 80 per cent of final salary. Employee contributions are tax-deductible. The pensionable age is generally 65 for men and 60 for women, although signs of increasing flexibility are becoming evident in this respect.

7.2.3 *Third pillar*

A special feature of pension arrangements in the third pillar is that they can be provided by both insurance companies and banks. Premiums are tax-deductible up to BEF 66,000, providing certain conditions are met: a minimum contract period of 10 years and a pensionable age of 65 for men and 60 for women. The tax benefit is based on an individual's average income tax rate, with a minimum of 30 per cent and a maximum of 40 per cent. Belgian tax legislation requires the life assurance company or bank providing the pension to be based in Belgium.

Premiums for capital sum insurance policies are not tax-deductible. Providing a policy can be defined as a life assurance policy and is for a minimum term of eight years and one month, the benefit will be paid out free of tax (even in the case of single-premium policies).

7.3 DENMARK

7.3.1 *First pillar*

The compulsory basic pension is financed on a PAYG basis from general government revenues, whilst supplementary occupational pensions are financed on a funded basis. The pension will be reduced by the amount of any earnings. No separate premiums are charged for the basic pension as it is financed from general government revenues. The premiums for supplementary pensions are paid two-thirds by the employer and one-third by the employee. The amount of the benefit is income-dependent and there is a maximum limit. All residents are entitled to receive a pension from the age of 67. An individual may defer retirement, either wholly or partially, at any time between the ages of 60 and 67. Early retirement is possible from the age of 50, albeit only on medical grounds. Those who have been a Danish resident for at least 40 years are entitled to receive a full pension, whilst the pensions of those who have been resident for less than 40 years will be reduced proportionately. Employees are only entitled to receive a supplementary pension if they have worked on a permanent basis between the ages of 16 and 66 for at least 10 hours per day. The supplementary pension is related to income earned during an individual's active working life. The average supplementary pension (for employees) is approximately 50 per cent of final salary.

7.3.2 Second pillar

In Denmark, the second pillar, which was originally only of importance for civil servants, has developed rapidly in recent years. Some 80 per cent of employees are now covered by occupational pension schemes, and in some sectors these are compulsory. Pensions are taxed when disbursed rather than whilst they are being built up. The benefits (18 per cent of total pension benefits) are largely financed on a funded basis and are administered by insurance companies and pension funds.[13] Premiums are usually paid jointly by employers and employees. The aim is to provide 60-70 per cent of final salary, excluding the first-pillar provisions. It should be pointed out that most pension schemes also pay out a capital sum on retirement date. The pensionable age is usually 65-67, but may be 60-62 in certain specific cases.

7.3.3 Third pillar

These retirement provisions, which are fully funded, are provided by insurance companies and banks. All premiums paid in respect of retirement provisions are taxed at a rate of 8 per cent. Premiums are normally deductible from income tax. A maximum of DKK 32,200 (1997) applies in the case of capital sum policies. This also applies to annuity premiums. The benefits paid out under a capital sum policy are taxed at 40 per cent, whilst annuity benefits are taxed at the progressive rate.

7.4 FINLAND

7.4.1 First pillar

First-pillar retirement provisions are financed on a PAYG basis and are designed to provide a pension to those without a supplementary pension or with a low basic income. All residents are insured from the age of 16. Employee premiums are paid partly by employers. There is no maximum cut-off threshold for contributions.

Anyone who has been a resident for 40 years between the age of 16 and retirement date is entitled to receive a pension. Shorter periods of residency will obviously result in a lower pension. The level of the pension depends on family circumstances, where an individual lives and on other pension benefits received.

The pensionable age for both men and women is 65. Early retirement is possible from the age of 60 (this involves a reduction in pension of 0.5 per

[13] It is also possible for individuals to set up their own occupational pension funds or to enter into an agreement with a bank. Little if any use is made of these opportunities.

cent for each month). Deferring retirement results in a pension increase of 1 per cent per month.

7.4.2 *Second pillar*

Employees are obliged to join a pension scheme.[14] There are separate arrangements for employees, temporary employees, freelancers, the self-employed, farmers and sailors. The arrangements vary from group to group. Pensions are built up at a rate of 1.5 per cent of pensionable salary each year, with account being taken of first-pillar pensions. Financing is partly on a funded basis and partly on a PAYG basis, with the exact proportion varying from occupational group to occupational group. The aim is to provide 60 per cent of final salary, and the taxation on disbursement rule applies. Some companies have voluntarily chosen to provide supplementary pensions of up to 66 per cent of final salary. The pensionable age is 65 for both men and women. Early retirement is possible from 60 years of age and entails a reduction in benefits of 5-6 per cent per year. Deferring a pension is rewarded with an increase of 1 per cent per month in benefits. Partial early retirement is possible.

7.4.3 *Third pillar*

Annuity premiums are tax-deductible. There are two ways of doing this: 10 per cent of salary is deductible providing benefits are not received before the age of 58. Alternatively, premiums of up to FIM 15,000 are fully deductible, with any premiums paid above that amount being deductible at 60 per cent, up to a maximum of FIM 30,000. The total amount deductible is, therefore, FIM 45,000 per year. If it can be shown that the first and second-pillar pension provisions represent less than 66 per cent of final salary, premiums of up to a maximum of FIM 50,000 per year may be deducted from tax.

With the exception of capital gains, benefits are taxed as income. Premiums paid on a capital sum policy are not tax-deductible. Benefits are taxed on a net basis at a rate of 28 per cent.

7.5 France

7.5.1 *First pillar*

In addition to a basic general pension, there are special schemes for certain groups (e.g. civil servants and the self-employed). Benefits are earnings-related. Insurance is compulsory for all employees. Premiums are divided between employers and employees (approximately 50/50). Employees receive a maximum of 50 per cent of average salary over the best 10 years of their working lives. There is a maximum cut-off salary of FRF 164,640 applying to the calculation of benefits, and contributions have to have been

[14] Five professions are covered by special regulations.

paid for at least 37.5 years. Any periods shorter than this will result in a lower pension. The pensionable age is 60 for both men and women. Early retirement is not possible.

7.5.2 *Second pillar*

All employees are obliged to join a pension scheme.[15] Some 90 per cent of employees in the private sector are covered by compulsory pension arrangements.[16] In addition to the compulsory schemes (financed on PAYG basis) there are also voluntary pension schemes (financed on a funded basis). Certain voluntary schemes (*Retraite à prestations definies*) may be managed by employers themselves, but contributions are not deductible from profits. These benefits comprise 21 per cent of total pension benefits. France applies the taxation on disbursement rule. There are also voluntary pension arrangements. Special entities have been entrusted with managing the compulsory pension schemes. Voluntary supplementary schemes can be operated by company pension funds or insurance companies. The level of benefits paid out under the compulsory arrangements depends on the number of pension points accumulated. Second-pillar benefits take no account of the state pension. Together, the first and second-pillar benefits usually amount to around 80 per cent of final salary. The pensionable age is 65 for both men and women. Early retirement is possible from the age of 60 under certain conditions. This does not reduce the level of the pension unless the individual has been insured for less than 40 years.

7.5.3 *Third pillar*

Since 1997, only life assurance premiums paid on a periodic basis have been tax-deductible. The maximum amount eligible for deduction is FRF 1,000 per family, plus FRF 250 per child. Social security premiums of 3.4 per cent are levied on the premiums paid. Since 1997 there has also been the opportunity for employees and the self-employed to make supplementary provisions for their old age.[17] Under these arrangements, individuals are entitled to an annuity upon retirement.

7.6 GERMANY

7.6.1 *First pillar*

The state pension scheme (*Renteversicherung)* forms the basis of the provisions. There are different schemes for the various sectors and professions and also various entities responsible for operating these. Except in the case of the self-employed and professional practitioners, pensions are financed on a PAYG basis. Premiums are paid jointly by employers and

---

[15] ARCO for non-managerial and managerial staff, AGIRC supplementary arrangements for managerial staff only.
[16] Green Paper p. 4.
[17] Loi Thomas and Loi Madelin.

employees, whilst the self-employed pay the full premium themselves. The pensionable age is 65 for both men and women, although early retirement is possible in certain circumstances (a long insured period). Women may retire at 60 and men at 63. In the event of early retirement, an individual's pension will be reduced by 3.6 per cent per year. Assuming an average insured period, gross benefits represent 43-50 per cent of final salary, whilst net benefits represent 62-70 per cent.

7.6.2 *Second pillar*

There is no general obligation to provide a pension, and pension schemes are not compulsory on a sectorial basis. At present, 46 per cent of employees (industry 66 per cent/trade 28 per cent) are covered by pension schemes. Most of these schemes are financed on a funded basis, but the substantial differences between the various schemes make it impossible to give a general indication of target levels of benefits. Second-pillar benefits represent 11 per cent of total pension benefits. There are no safeguards in the sense of requiring pensions to be administered by specific entities. The official pensionable age is 65, but early retirement is possible. Second-pillar benefits take no account of the state pension.

A distinction is drawn in Germany between:

- *Direktzusagen* (54 per cent), which involve provisions for pension commitments being made in the balance sheet. This method can best be described as self-administration. The full risk is borne by the employer. The way this method is treated from a tax perspective–the provisions are tax-deductible–means it is a popular option. This type of pension is taxed on disbursement rather than whilst it is being built up; and
- *Unterstützungskassen* (13 per cent), *Pensionskassen* (19 per cent) and *Direktversicherung* (14 per cent). Employers may deduct their contributions to such schemes from tax, whilst employees are taxed (i.e. the taxation on disbursement rule does not apply) up to a maximum of DEM 3,000 (or DEM 4,200 in certain specific cases) at a rate of 15 per cent.

7.6.3 *Third pillar*

Life assurance premiums (both capital sum and annuity policies) with a term of at least 12 years may be deducted from tax. Benefits paid out under a capital sum policy are tax-free. The interest component of annuities is taxed. This is calculated using actuarial tables, with the starting date and the term of the benefits being the determining factors. Benefits paid out upon the death of an insured individual are tax-free.

7.7 NORWAY

7.7.1 First pillar

The pension in the first pillar, which is financed on a PAYG basis, provides both earnings-related benefits and benefits which are independent of income. It is compulsory, both for employees and the self-employed. Paying premiums for 40 years entitles an individual to a full non-earnings-related pension. Employers and employees are jointly responsible for paying the premiums, whereas the self-employed pay their own premiums in full. If premiums are paid for fewer than 40 years, a reduced pension will be received. Pension points need to be accumulated over a period of at least three years in order for an individual to be entitled to a supplementary, earnings-related pension. The premiums depend on such things as the region in which an individual lives. There is no maximum cut-off for premiums. The self-employed pay the premiums themselves, whilst employee premiums are paid partly by the employer.

The pensionable age is 67 for both men and women. With the exception of a number of special groups such as civil servants, early retirement is not possible because of the costs this would entail. Retirement may be deferred until the age of 70 at the latest.

7.7.2 Second pillar

More and more pension schemes have been established in the last 30 years. Approximately half of Norwegian employees are members of a pension scheme. Usually, the employer pays the premiums. Public servants and local government employees receive pensions representing two-thirds of earnings, and these are financed partly on a funded and partly on a PAYG basis. Most pension schemes aim to provide 60-66 per cent of final salary (including the first-pillar pension), but some set out to provide 70 per cent. All other pensions are financed on a funded basis. Early retirement is possible from the age of 64.

7.7.3 Third pillar

Premiums for private pension plans are tax-deductible up to a maximum of 10 per cent of the previous year's earnings, with a maximum of NOK 30,000. The benefits received are fully taxable.

7.8 SPAIN

7.8.1 First pillar

A distinction is made in the first pillar between the basic state pension and the supplementary pension available to certain groups in the workforce. Both systems are financed on a PAYG basis. The basic pension is earnings-related, whereas the supplementary scheme is not. Insurance is compulsory for employees and the self-employed. The pensionable age for both men and women is 65. Early retirement is possible from the age of 60 (this involves a reduction of 8 per cent per year in pension benefits). Deferred retirement is also possible (this results in an increase of 2 per cent for each year).

7.8.2 *Second pillar*

Supplementary pension schemes, operated by life assurance companies and pension funds on a funded basis, are voluntary and are now becoming ever more common.[18] A total of 15 per cent of employees are covered by a second-pillar scheme. Benefits represent 3 per cent of total pension benefits. Employers are entitled in principle to undertake to provide pensions to certain employees. Premiums are paid by the employer. The pensionable age is 65 for both men and women.

The taxation on disbursement rule does not apply in the event of the employer deducting the cost of the premiums from profits. If premiums are deducted, the pension claim will be taxed and the benefits will be disbursed tax-free. Second-pillar provisions take no account of the state pension.

7.8.3 *Third pillar*

There are limited fiscal stimuli in respect of third-pillar provisions. Of the premiums paid, 10 per cent is deductible from income tax.

7.9 SWITZERLAND

7.9.1 *First pillar*

The state pension is financed on a PAYG basis and guarantees a minimum income, with benefits dependent on earnings during an individual's active working life. All residents are compulsorily insured from the age of 18. The pensionable age is 65 for men and 62 for women. There is no maximum cut-off for premiums. Employers and employees each pay half of the premium, which amounts to 8.4 per cent of salary. The self-employed pay 7.8 per cent, whilst the state contributes 19.6 per cent of the total cost.

The level of benefits depends on the premiums paid and the average earnings of the insured individual. In 1995, the single person's pension amounted to a maximum of CHF 23,280, with married couples receiving 150 per cent of the single person's pension.

7.9.2 *Second pillar*

Pensions are compulsory, and employers are obliged to undertake to provide pensions on salary amounts between CHF 23,280 and CHF 69,840 (1997). Life and invalidity insurance are compulsory from the age of 17. Retirement pensions are compulsory from the age of 24. The aim is to provide 60 per cent of average salaries (this includes the state pension).

---

[18] Since 1995 it has been compulsory for pension commitments to be held outside the company undertaking to provide the pension.

Pensions are financed on a funded basis and the taxation on disbursement rule applies. The state pension is taken account of in occupational pension schemes.

There are also voluntary pension arrangements available. The pensionable age is 62 for women and 65 for men. Early (maximum: five years) and deferred retirement are both possible. The taxation on disbursement rule applies.

7.9.3 *Third pillar*

A distinction is made in the third pillar between tied (*Gebundene Vorsorge*) and free (*Freie Selbstvorsorge*) arrangements. Premiums for the former (schemes operated by a bank or insurance company) are deductible up to a maximum of CHF 5,587 for individuals covered by the second pillar and up to a maximum of 20 per cent of income or CHF 27,936 for those not covered by second-pillar provisions (i.e. the self-employed). Benefits paid out under *Gebundene Vorsorge* arrangements are taxed at a reduced rate, whilst benefits paid out under *Freie Selbstvorsorge* schemes are taxed at 60 per cent.

7.10 UNITED KINGDOM

7.10.1 *First pillar*

There is a basic state pension scheme and also a supplementary scheme (state earnings-related pension scheme, or SERPS). The former comprises a non-earnings-related basic pension, whilst the latter is related to earnings. All employees and self-employed people are covered by the basic scheme, and all employees are also compulsorily insured under the SERPS scheme. It is possible, however, to contract out of SERPS. The self-employed are not entitled to join SERPS, even on a voluntary basis. SERPS benefits are equivalent to 25 per cent of a maximum earnings level set by law. Premiums are payable by employers and employees.

The pensionable age is 65 for men and 60 for women. Between 2010 and 2020 the pensionable age for women is being raised gradually to 65. Early retirement is not possible. Deferred retirement is, however, possible and results in a pension increase of 7.5 per cent per year.

7.10.2 *Second pillar*

Companies can operate different pension schemes for different groups of employees. Membership of a scheme set up voluntarily by an employer can no longer be made compulsory as it has been possible to opt out since 1988. As a result, pensions are now fully portable.

Most pension schemes are financed on a funded basis. Benefits based on final salaries usually represent two-thirds of the final salary. In practice, most employees receive a lower pension. The taxation on disbursement rule is applied. Second-pillar provisions take account of the state pension. The tendency in respect of the pensionable age is to follow the line set for the first pillar: 65 for men and 60 for women. Early retirement is possible from the age of 50.

7.10.3 *Third pillar*

Personal pension schemes in the third pillar can generally be arranged via insurance companies, banks and housing corporations. In the event of a decision to opt out (in the second pillar), the Social Security Ministry will pay part of the premium. The level of contributions are age- and earnings-related and vary from 20-40 per cent. The maximum salary on which contributions can be paid is GBP 84,000. Contributions are tax-free, as is the capital gain during the term of the policy. Benefits are regarded as taxable income. Premiums paid in respect of capital sum policies or annuities are not tax-deductible.

8 First Steps Towards a European Union Solution

The impact of the decisions of the ECJ becomes ever bigger. The Member States cannot pass over those decisions. The Dutch fiscal regulations relating to pensions could be the key to harmonisation at a European Union level. The Netherlands has the most liberal system. Also the possibilities for transfer of the worth of pension rights and continuation of pensions and life-annuities built up in other countries after immigration is well developed, compared with the situation in other Member States. A solution to the obstacles highlighted could be achieved via a Regulation. Using bilateral treaties as a means to ensure that adequate measures are taken would seem to me to be too laborious and time-consuming. According to the Green Paper, there would be 105 bilateral treaties needing to be amended.

A Regulation would have to establish the following basic assumptions and principles:

- the general principle of the taxation on disbursement rule (*nachgelagte Besteuerung*) in the case of pensions;
- the deductibility of premiums from profits;
- the principle that if the treaty assigns earned income to the country in which an individual works, that country will also be obliged to treat income used by a non-resident to pay annuity premiums in the same way as income used by resident tax-payers;
- the principle of benefits being taxable, with a minimum tariff being set;
- abolition in certain circumstances of the requirement in national legislation for the pension administrator/life assurance company to be based in the specific country;
- definitions of terms, criteria and minimum specifications for pensions, fiscally approved pension schemes and annuities; clearer guidance will be needed on such issues as those individuals

entitled to receive benefits and the question of commutation (full, partial or not at all);

- value transfers to a tax-approved pension scheme should be straightforward from a fiscal perspective; in order to avoid pension migration and to ensure that a transfer value is only possible when an individual changes jobs, it will have to be stipulated that such should only be allowed in the event of an individual *remaining in employment*;
- the obligation to exchange information and the procedures for this.

The above will make it possible for pension arrangements to be managed/ continued by an entity in another Member State. Clearly, many and maybe all the Member States will have to be prepared to make concessions as there are currently significant differences in both the nature of pension schemes and the fiscal legislation in the Member States. One possibility would perhaps be for a Member State to be allowed, for example, to pay out part of the pension reserve in one go on the retirement date. In this respect, the Belgian and UK traditions particularly are different from those in the Netherlands.

Effective means of exchanging information between the various Member States would be a prerequisite. Similarly, the Member States would have to commit themselves to levying a reasonable rate of tax on benefits (within a band of rates specified in the Regulation).[19] What obviously cannot be allowed to happen is a Member State only levying tax on pension benefits received if premiums were deducted from income whilst the pension was being built up in the current country of residence.

The same system could be used for annuities. I should emphasise here that the fiscal rules and regulations applying to annuities differ even more between the Member States than those governing pensions. For example, 70 per cent is more or less the general norm for pensions in most of the Member States, whereas there is in effect no norm or target level for annuities. The Dutch tranche system is recognised as being at the forefront of developments in Europe. In the case of capital sum policies, a uniform definition of life assurance would first need to be established. The second step could then be to align the various fiscal methods for paying out benefits free of tax.

---

19 Another possibility could be for set-off arrangements to be agreed between the country of residence and the country which had allowed the income to be deferred in the past. Such a system would not appear to me to be easy to administer. Moreover, there are no examples of such a system in the current treaty network.

9 Conclusions

- Despite the fact that pension systems vary significantly from country to country, there are also certain similarities. For example, almost all countries finance their state pension schemes (first pillar) on a PAYG basis. In contrast, pensions in the second pillar and private provisions in the third pillar are either largely or exclusively financed on a funded basis.
- Pension benefits represent taxable income. A number of countries do make a distinction between recurrent benefits and lump-sum benefits. In the United Kingdom, for example, a lump-sum payment is untaxed (up to a limited amount), whilst in Spain it is taxed more heavily than recurrent benefits. In certain countries, pension arrangements require prior approval. This is the case in Austria, Switzerland, Germany, Spain, United Kingdom and Norway.
- There are only a few countries where the tax treatment of premiums paid to a pension manager abroad is less favourable than the tax treatment of premiums paid to a pension manager based in the home country. This is the case in Belgium, Denmark, Finland and Norway.
- Occupational pensions are only compulsory in a limited number of countries: Switzerland, Finland, France and Norway. Although occupational pensions are not compulsory in the Netherlands, 91 per cent of employees are actually covered by such arrangements.
- The Netherlands is the only country in Europe where the employer has to fund pension commitments in full when an employee leaves the company. Finland is the only country where a transfer value is not available when an employee changes jobs.[20] Almost all countries do, however, make the transfer subject to certain conditions. The idea behind these conditions is that the nature of the pension should remain unchanged and that the entity taking over responsibility for the pension should be an authorised pension administrator.
- Almost all countries grant tax privileges to encourage individuals to make supplementary provisions. These either involve premiums being deductible or benefits being disbursed free of tax.
- The level of coverage in the second pillar varies greatly and is largely determined by the extent of cover provided in the first pillar and whether or not pensions are compulsory.
- Switzerland has taken the three-pillar system the furthest, at least in terms of linking the provisions of the different pillars.

---

[20] This is not shown in the overview of the various countries, but has been taken from the CEA survey in June 1997 entitled *System of occupational pension provision and the tax treatment thereof.*

- The Netherlands is one of the best countries in terms of pensions. Pension provisions in the Netherlands, whether in the first pillar (numbers of insured individuals, earnings-related), second pillar (high level of coverage and high target levels) or the third pillar (generous tax facilities), may be regarded as some of the best in the European Union.

10 Tables

Table 1a First pillar: state pensions provisions

State pension	*Insured*	*Financing*	*Payment of premiums*
Austria	Employees and self-employed	PAYG	Employers and employees - approx. 50/50
Belgium	Employees, civil servants, self-employed	PAYG, except for civil servants	Employer/ employee No maximum
Denmark	All residents	Basic pension: PAYG from general govt. revenues. Supplementary employee benefits: funded basis	Basic pension: from general revenues Supplementary pension: 2/3 employer and 1/3 employee up to specified maximum
Finland	All residents	PAYG	Employers/ employees No maximum
France	Employees, civil servants, self-employed	PAYG	Employers/ employees up to specified maximum
Germany	Civil servants, employees, sailors and certain self-employed groups and professions	PAYG, except for professionals	Employers/ employees Self-employed: whole premium
Netherlands	All residents	PAYG	Premium paid in full by individuals over the first NLG 45,960 (1997)
Norway	Employees and self-employed	PAYG	Employers and employees

Table 1a First pillar: state pensions provisions (continued)

State pension	*Insured*	*Financing*	*Payment of premiums*
Spain	Employees and self-employed	PAYG	Employers and employees up to specified maximum
Switzerland	All residents	PAYG	Employers and employees - 50/50
United Kingdom	Employees and self-employed	PAYG	Employers and employees

Table 1b First pillar: state pensions benefits

State pension	*Pensionable age*	*Early retirement possible*	*Benefits earnings-related/ Dependent on pension*
Austria	65 (m), 60 (w)	Early and deferred retirement possible Partial retirement possible	Earnings-related
Belgium	60-65	From 60	Yes Earnings-related
Denmark	67	Partial retirement possible between 60 and 67	Supplementary pension: earnings-related
Finland	65	From 60, reduction in benefits of 0.5% per month	Benefit dependent on where individual lives, family circumstances and pension
France	60	Early retirement not possible	Benefits are independent of income, but earnings-related
Germany	65 (m), 60 (w)	Yes	Earnings-related
Italy	60(m), 55 (w)*		
Netherlands	65	No	Life/non-earnings-related
Norway	67	Early retirement not possible Deferred retirement possible	Earnings-related
Spain	65	Early retirement possible from 60: reduction of 8% per annum Deferred retirement: increase of 2% per annum	Basic pension: non-earnings-related Supplementary pension: earnings-related
Switzerland	65 (m), 62 (w)	Early (2 years/ reduction of 6.8%) and deferred retirement are possible (increase of 5.2% per annum).	Earnings-related
United Kingdom	65 (m), 60 (w)	Early retirement not possible	Basic pension: non-earnings-related SERPS: earnings-related

* Steps were recently taken to raise the pensionable age in Italy.

Table 2a Second pillar: occupational pensions arrangements

Occupational pensions	*Are pensions compulsory?*	*Supplementary, compulsory arrangements for groups of employees/ sectors*	*Voluntary arrangements*
Austria	No	No	Yes
Belgium	No	No	Yes
Denmark	No	No	Yes
Finland	Yes	Yes, equivalent to general, compulsory pensions	Yes
France	Yes	No	Yes
Germany	No	No	Yes
Ireland			
Italy	No		
Netherlands	No	Yes	Yes
Norway	No	No	Yes
Spain	No	No	Yes
Switzerland	Yes	No	Yes
United Kingdom	No	No	Yes

Table 2b Second pillar: occupational pensions provisions

Occupational pensions	*Method of financing*	*Form of commitment*	*Account taken of state pension*
Austria	Funded basis		No
Belgium	Partly PAYG and partly funded basis	Usually 60% of final salary	Yes
Denmark	Largely funded basis	60-70 % of final salary	No
Finland	Partly PAYG and partly funded basis	60% of final salary, and up to 66% in certain exceptional cases	Yes
France	Compulsory schemes: PAYG Voluntary schemes: funded basis	Usually 80% of final salary	No
Germany	Self-administered and funded basis	No clear line	No
Netherlands	Funded basis	Mainly 70% of final salary Increasing number of schemes based on average salary	Yes
Norway	Partly PAYG and partly funded basis	60-66% of final salary	Yes
Spain	Funded basis	No information available in Spain on levels	No
Switzerland	Funded basis	60% of average salary	Yes
United Kingdom	Mainly funded basis	2/3 of final salary	No

Table 2c Second pillar: occupational pensions benefits

Occupational pensions	*Pensionable age*	*Taxation on disbursement rule*	*Extent of cover*
Austria	65(m), 60 (w)	Yes	Low
Belgium	65(m), 60 (w) Increasing flexibility	Yes, limited to 80%	
Denmark	Between 65 and 67	Yes	80%
Finland	65 Early retirement possible from 60	Yes	X
France	65 Early retirement possible	Yes	90%
Germany	65 Early retirement possible	Depends on commitments	Industry 66% Trade 28%
Netherlands	65 Early retirement becoming possible	Yes	91%
Norway	Early retirement possible from 64	Yes	50%
Spain	X	No, if employers deduct premiums from profits	15%
Switzerland	65(m), 62 (w)	Yes	100% employees
United Kingdom	65(m), 60 (w) Early retirement often possible from age of 50	Yes	X

Movement of Persons in Europe: Tax, Pensions and Social Security[1]

Peter Kavelaars

Professor of Tax Law at the Erasmus University Rotterdam and at the University of Leiden, and Director of Research of Deloitte & Touche Tax Advisors in Rotterdam

1 Introduction

Labour is becoming an increasingly mobile factor, and this trend looks certain to continue. Not only has it become very unusual for employees to spend their whole working lives with one employer, but it is now commonplace for many employees to work abroad for short or long periods and/or on several different occasions. The reasons for this are the growing internationalisation of the business sector in general and–in the case of the European Union–the creation of the single market in particular. It is rare for complications to arise in respect of applicable legislation when the periods abroad are of a relatively short duration; what individuals may well come across are special facilities which are usually designed to cover some of the additional costs commonly associated with working abroad; the

---

[1] This text is very similar to the text of the presentation given by the author to mark his appointment as Professor of Taxation Law at the University of Leiden on 13 March 1998. The Dutch-language version, *Harmonisatie van vrij personenverkeer: een drieluik,* is published by Kluwer, Deventer, 1998.

so-called *Nedeco* ruling[2] and the 35 per cent ruling[3] are obvious examples of these in a Dutch context (these facilities involve a set concession designed to cover the additional costs with which employees seconded abroad may have to contend); these facilities may also apply in the case of a more lengthy period abroad.[4] Alongside facilities of this nature, there are three primary issues facing those working in cross-border situations. These are:

1. is the income taxable and, if so, where?
2. are social security contributions payable and, if so, where?
3. can a pension be built up, and is tax relief available on contributions? If so, where and how are the benefits taxed?

In this chapter I will be examining these issues and I will show that there are substantial differences between the various national and international regulations in a number of areas. These can cause a range of complications, and this is obviously undesirable within the single market. In essence, there are two types of difference. First, the various legislative systems are structured differently. Secondly, the rules on assigning levying powers in respect of tax, social security and pensions differ from country to country. This is an undesirable situation, both from the perspective of the individual working in a cross-border situation and from the employer or customer's point of view. It is striking, furthermore, that there are few if any reasons why certain assignment rules are as they are. That is true both for tax and social security. Since there are in effect no international pension assignment rules, there is obviously no reasoning here either.

Before analysing the differences and similarities between the various assignment rules relating to the specific categories of activities and persons, I will first discuss the fundamental principles on which the international fiscal, social security and pension rules and regulations are based.

2 Basic Assumptions

2.1 Taxation

The most important basic assumption in terms of assigning the right to levy tax in an international context concerns the nature of the income, i.e. the object. This means it is impossible to link levying powers to the individual,

---

[2] Decree of 17 January 1995, IFZ94/1042, BNB 1995/84.

[3] Decrees of 4 June 1992, DB92/922, BNB 1992/284 and 28 August 1992, DB92/4418, BNB 1992/331.

[4] In this respect, the two rulings differ significantly: the 35 per cent ruling is only applicable to those liable to pay tax in the Netherlands, which will normally mean a period of residence longer than 183 days. Treaties will often be involved, although this need not necessarily be the case. The *Nedeco* ruling, on the other hand, is far more frequently relevant in cases involving secondments, usually for a shorter period, to non-treaty countries.

i.e. the subject. This line has normally been followed consistently in national legislative systems. In the treaty network, however, this is not the case. The way the treaties have been formulated partly reflects the nature of the income (e.g. income generated from activities in self-employment or on the basis of paid employment) and partly the type of persons involved (e.g. income earned as a director or as an employee in public service). In material terms, however, these international regulations also mean that ultimately it is the object that determines which country is assigned the right to levy charges since the sole issue at stake is the specific activity generating the income. European law provisions are of absolutely no relevance in this respect.

Basing the assignment on the object rather than the subject means that two or more countries may be entitled to levy tax in the event of cross-border activities being performed. This is also an extension of the widely accepted principle of demarcation, i.e. the country of residence principle and the source country principle. The double liability for taxation this creates for the subject gives rise to the need for measures to prevent double taxation; these take the form of a reduction in the amount of tax payable by means of set-off or the granting of exemptions.

The most significant features of the system used in the tax world are, therefore:

- the assignment of the right to levy tax is related to the object;
- a subject may be obliged to pay tax in more than one country;
- specific methods are used to determine the amount of tax due in each of the countries.

2.2 SOCIAL SECURITY

In contrast to fiscal legislation, European rules and regulations[5] are of great importance in a European Union social security context in respect of assigning the duty to levy social security premiums. A number of social security treaties have also been signed with countries outside the European Union. These are, however, far fewer in number than the tax treaties, and they are generally of limited importance.[6] There is no standard treaty used as a model in the field of international social security.[7] Nevertheless–and in contrast to fiscal legislation–there are a number of supranational and

[5] Regulation 1408/71 and the implementation Regulation 574/72.

[6] The limited importance arises on the one hand from the fact that the treaties signed between Member States of the European Union are now to a large extent insignificant since these have generally been replaced by Regulation 1408/71. The other treaties are limited in number and in some cases have been entered into with countries with which there are only limited economic ties. It is noteworthy, for example, that there is no social security treaty with Japan. Similarly, I find it strange that the Netherlands has made no arrangements in this respect with the Netherlands Antilles or Aruba.

[7] Nevertheless, the structures of the various treaties are to a large extent comparable; the rules contained in the treaties are also very similar.

international treaties which are applicable.[8] In addition, national legislative systems contain a relatively large number of special rules[9] specifically relating to social security in an international context, and these are all exceptions to the basic rules.

The most important feature of the various treaties is that they all essentially focus on the benefits side. The demarcation of compulsory national insurance–in effect, it is a matter of assigning this obligation–is only covered to a limited degree. Moreover, the treaties only rarely contain provisions specifically relating to the levying of premiums. This is mainly because in the case of social security it is a matter of compulsory national insurance and the assigning of responsibility for it, and this affects both the benefits/disbursements side and the premiums side.[10] How the rights and obligations are then interpreted is a matter for national legislation.

The most significant features of social security legislation in European law are as follows:

- the obligation to participate in a national insurance scheme is subject rather than object-related;[11]
- the insurance obligation is in principle always assigned to one country to the exclusion of another country. This exclusivity principle is more or less a logical extension of the fact that the insurance obligation is subject-related;[12]
- the insurance obligation can only be assigned to a country if the

---

8 In addition to Regulation 1408/71 and Regulation 574/72 the most important ones are the Council of Europe's social security convention, the Rhine Navigators Convention *(Rijnvarendenverdrag)* and the Transportation Convention *(Transportverdrag)*. For more information see: P. Kavelaars, *Toewijzingsregels in het Europees sociaal-verzekeringsrecht* (Deventer: Kluwer, 1992), p. 132 ff.

9 Decree on the expansion and restriction of those covered by national insurance 1989, Stb. 1989, 164 and the Decree on the expansion and restriction of those covered by employed persons insurance schemes Stb. 1990, 402.

10 The Supreme Court decision of 8 July 1997, 31 540, BNB 1997/310c* to the effect that, based on the principle of strong effect, Regulation 1408/71 results in compulsory national insurance and the right to benefits without any obligation to pay contributions should in my opinion be regarded as obviously incorrect. For a discussion of the decision in this case I refer to my comments in the above BNB and my article 'Bewegelijkheid in het Europees sociaal verzekeringsrecht' in *WFR* 1997/6272, 1791-1804. That the principle of strong effect affects both the benefits side and the levying side is obvious for a variety of reasons. First, a Member State could never agree to a situation in which it might have to face paying benefits without any right to levy premiums. Secondly, the other country which is a party to the treaty will normally not or not be able to levy premiums in such cases; the levying powers will, therefore, fall between two stools. Lastly, it can be concluded from previous decisions by the ECJ that the principle of strong effect also applies on the levying side; see the publication referred to above for more information. The subsequent amendment of the law has since nullified the result of this decision.

11 Although the nature of the object may well influence which country is ultimately assigned.

12 There are a number of exceptions to this principle within the European Union. These are specified in Regulation 1408/71, Appendix VII. It is not specified whether or not bilateral treaties are also based on the exclusivity principle.

legislation of the relevant Member State allows for this or if the legislation specifically does not allow for it in that the country of residence principle is applied. In the latter case, the insurance obligation arises on the basis of the principle of strong effect.[13]

One result of the above rules is that methods designed to prevent premiums being charged twice are more or less insignificant in the case of social security; only in exceptional circumstances will such methods need to be applied, and these cases will not be discussed here.

A comparison of the basic assumptions on tax with those on social security shows the following:

- the duty to pay tax is usually in two countries, whereas the obligation to pay social security premiums is normally only in one;
- in the case of social security, the country of residence criterion is not applied in many cases. This is not so in respect of tax;
- the various tax treaties include methods to determine how tax relief should be granted in order to prevent double taxation; such methods are rarely if ever seen in social security treaties;
- there are far fewer categories of persons in the fiscal sphere to whom assignment rules apply than there are in the social security sphere;
- the types of income covered by assignment rules for tax purposes are only seen to a very limited degree in respect of social security;
- where comparable rules of assignment exist in a general sense, the conditions and criteria are frequently neither the same nor comparable.

2.3 Pensions

2.3.1 Introduction

There are no treaties in the field of pensions legislation. This means that, in principle, only national legislation can determine what happens. Nevertheless, there have been a number of European Life Assurance directives which are of relevance to pensions in an international context. In addition, a European Pensions Directive is currently being worked on. The reason for the absence of treaties is largely due to the fact that pensions are not normally compulsory, in contrast to taxation and social security premiums. Moreover, pension arrangements are generally subject to private or semi-private law, whilst fiscal and social security legislation[14] are public law issues. The various rules and regulations of relevance to pensions in an international context are discussed below in more detail.

---

13 Whether and to what extent this principle is of relevance in other treaties is not clear.

14 In view of the partial privatisation of the social security system, this is no longer completely true.

2.3.2 *Some general aspects at a national level*

Pensions, too, are covered by legislation at both national and international level. One significant difference *viz-à-viz* the areas of law referred to above is, however, the fact that there are absolutely no treaties on the subject of pensions. Indeed, the international regulations comprise 'only' the three life assurance directives,[15] of which only the third is in effect still of significance since it has replaced the first two directives. In addition, a pensions directive is currently being worked on.[16] Of specific importance for fiscal aspects of international pensions is the OECD Model Convention, Article 18 and the related commentary.

At a national, Dutch level, there are hardly any specific rules relating to international pensions, either in respect of the building up of pensions or the paying out of pension benefits. This is hardly surprising since the residence of former employees has no bearing on their right to receive pensions: they are always entitled to their pensions.[17] In fact, only the Pension and Savings Funds Act, Article 2 contains a rule on which a general conclusion can be based; when evaluating this it is important primarily to realise that the Pension and Savings Funds Act has a completely different objective from that of the fiscal and social security legislation. The basic issue in the case of the Pension and Savings Funds Act is whether or not pension arrangements are protected by law. The Act cannot, therefore, contain guidelines and/or principles. There is no specific link to an object or subject. Neither does the Act cover methods designed to prevent the double levying of premiums. The Pension and Savings Funds Act, Article 2 states that pension arrangements are in principle protected by the Pension and Savings Funds Act unless the employee lives and works abroad. See section 2.3.3 below.

Another provision of relevance to this issue in an international context is the rule on commutation: non-residents have slightly more opportunities to commute pensions.[18] Furthermore, pension capital may also be transferred abroad under certain conditions. Transfers normally relate to international transfer values for individuals accepting employment abroad; the availability of tax relief is very much geared towards these types of situation. Thirdly, the Regulation of Insurance Contracts, Article 2a is important; a

---

15 First Directive 79/267/EEC of 5 March 1979; Second Directive 90/619/EEC of 8 November 1990; Third Directive 92/96/EEC of 10 November 1992.

16 Draft Pensions Directive of 19 November 1997, OJ 1997 C5, 9 January 1998. See also Green Paper, *Supplementary Pensions in the Single Market* (June 1997). Essentially, this Green Paper develops further the discussion started in the Working Document published in 1994 on cross-border pensions, *Grensoverschrijdende deelneming aan bedrijfspensioenregelingen voor migrerende werknemers*, no. XV/2040/92 of 21 October 1992. The said Draft Pensions Directive should not be confused with a previous draft pensions directive, which mainly focused on achieving greater harmonisation of pension funds' activities.

17 This is of course completely logical since it involves a legally enforceable right. The right to pension benefits is in principle no different from the right to receive the basic state pension (AOW): this right, too, can never be lost.

18 Pension and Savings Funds Act, Article 32(5).

decision by an insured individual to the effect that the pension arrangements should be governed by a law other than Dutch law is not allowed to impact on the applicability or otherwise of the Pension and Savings Funds Act. The purpose of this is to ensure that it is not possible to circumvent the Pension and Savings Funds Act, specifically in respect of the prohibition on pension commutation. This regulation would not appear to be very effective, either from a legal or actual perspective.[19] Lastly, the Pension and Savings Funds Act, Article 29 is important in this context: on the one hand it provides for an exemption from the applicability of the Pension and Savings Funds Act, whilst on the other hand it makes it possible for voluntary pension arrangements to be covered by the Act.

2.3.3 *Building up pensions*

In the Pension and Savings Funds Act, the main issue in respect of pensions being built up is to determine which specific cases are covered by the legislation. Only then is it possible for pension rights to be safeguarded. In the absence of a relationship with the Netherlands during the time that a pension is being built up the Pension and Savings Funds Act obviously cannot be applicable. The question is, however, what is the minimal relationship needed for the Pension and Savings Funds Act[20] to apply. Only Article 2(3)(b) of the Act gives any indication in the sense that, in contrast to the basic rule of the first subsection, it states that the Pension and Savings Funds Act does not apply to:

- employees working outside the Netherlands, or
- employees taken on for the purposes of performing work outside the Netherlands.

In both cases, the exclusion does not apply in the event of the individual being resident in the Netherlands. The Pension and Savings Funds Act does not contain any special provisions for special cases such as frontier employees or seconded employees, although employers can be granted dispensations for employees seconded to the Netherlands by other members of the same group.[21] The position of the employer is irrelevant; in other words, it makes no difference whether the employer is located in the Netherlands or elsewhere. In this respect, the approach seen in the

---

19 The effectiveness and legal significance of Regulation of Insurance Contracts, Article 2a are discussed specifically in P. van Huizen, 'Afkoopverbod: grensoverschrijdend?' *Pensioen & Praktijk* 1994/10, 10-13 and W.M.A. Kalkman, 'Afkoopverbod: grensoverschrijdend!' *Pensioen & Praktijk* 1994/12, 17-20 (with postscript by Van Huizen).

20 Neither the Dutch Company Pension Fund (Obligatory Participation) Act nor the Occupational Pension Fund (Obligatory Participation) Act contain any provisions specifically relating to cross-border situations. The Insurance Industry (Supervision) Act 1993 also contains no relevant provisions in respect of the positions of the employer and employee. For more information, see E. Lutjens, *Pensioenvoorzieningen voor werknemers* (Zwolle: Tjeenk Willink, 1989), pp. 109-112.

21 Pension and Savings Funds Act, Article 29(3), juncto Dispensation Decree, Article 2(1)(e).

Pension and Savings Funds Act is in line with that of the employee insurance schemes, where the location of the employer is also of no importance. This means, for example, that a pension undertaken to be provided by a non-Dutch employer will only fall outside the scope of the Pension and Savings Funds Act in the event of the employee residing and working outside the Netherlands. It is particularly interesting that–in the case of a non-Dutch employer–the Pension and Savings Funds Act will apply to the pension commitments even if the employee only resides or only works in the Netherlands. In this respect, therefore, the Pension and Savings Funds Act goes further than the employee insurance schemes. This approach is not particularly logical: first because this legislation could easily conflict with, for example, legislation in the country in which the employer is based. If the laws of that country require pension commitments to be made there, the only recourse will be to international private law.[22] In cases such as this, the result will often be that it is the other country's pension legislation which applies rather than the Pension and Savings Funds Act. If the non-Dutch employer were effectively to be subject to the Pension and Savings Funds Act, it would mean that the pension commitments would actually have to be held in the Netherlands; notwithstanding the Third Life Assurance Directive, which states that pensions are in principle allowed to be held with any insurer established in a European Union country, the Wages and Salaries Tax Act 1964, Article 19a states that pension commitments must be included in the calculation of a company's domestic company capital; this also of course applies to Dutch branches of foreign insurance companies.[23]

2.3.4 *General developments at a European level*

There have been a number of developments at a European level in supplementary pensions legislation, with the first of these being the issue of a Working Document in 1994. In 1997 a Green Paper was issued, and this formed the basis for the draft Directive on supplementary pensions. Alongside these developments, some of which have still to take final shape and will not yet, therefore, have come into effect, three European Life Assurance Directives have also been issued. The Third Life Assurance Directive, which came into effect in 1994, takes the subject furthest and, therefore, effectively replaces the first two Life Assurance Directives. The effect of the Third Life Assurance Directive is that there should be no obstacles to prevent insurance companies from operating beyond their national boundaries. One way of doing this is to establish a branch or subsidiary in a country other than the home country of the parent company and then to provide services from that host country. Another way is to

---

[22] Unless an exemption can be obtained.

[23] The decision in Case C-240/90 *Bachman* [1992] ECR 249 (28 January 1992, ECJ), referred to again below, suggests that this requirement probably does not contravene European law. The decision in Case C-118/96 *Safir* (28 April 1998, ECJ) suggests a modification of the decision in the *Bachman* case, but the position is not really very clear.

provide services directly from the original home country rather than via a branch or subsidiary in a host country. This freedom to provide services arises directly from Article 59 et seq. of the EC Treaty. What is important in this context is that the insurer is not required to comply with the life assurance legislation of the country in which its branch or subsidiary is located; neither is the insurer required to comply with the conditions applying in the specific Member State in the event of services being provided directly from the insurance company's home country. In principle, therefore, there are no obstacles standing in the way of the freedom to provide services. Nevertheless, there are two factors which can affect this freedom:

1. The Life Assurance Directives do not apply to pension funds. Treating pension funds differently from life assurance companies would seem to me to be very undesirable, given the fact that they are competitors; in effect, competition is being distorted. This means in the case of the Netherlands that B and C policy pensions are covered by the Third Life Assurance Directive, whilst pensions provided by pension funds are not.
2. The Life Assurance Directives allow Member States to decide for themselves whether or not tax relief should be granted on pensions in cross-border situations.

The latter aspect in particular is obviously very important in cases where Member States choose to make tax relief available on pensions being built up. In such cases, it is not unusual for tax relief to be restricted to the country in which the pension has been built up (see above). Clearly, this type of restriction will certainly impact on the building up of pensions in cross-border situations. In the cases of those Member States not granting tax relief on pension provisions (see below) there is obviously nothing to prevent individuals from building up pensions in another country.

In addition to the Life Assurance Directives, the Working Document, Green Paper and Draft Pensions Directive have also been mentioned; essentially, these all set out to remove obstacles to the creation of pension provisions in cross-border situations. There are various types of obstacle, for example:

- private law stipulations on the cross-border building up and transfer of pensions;[24]
- differences in types of pension arrangement;
- different conditions for life assurance companies (this aspect is of only limited significance since the introduction of the three Life Assurance Directives);

[24] Other examples of obstacles could be waiting periods that have to be observed before an individual is allowed to join a pension scheme or conditions to the effect that pension claims will be forfeited in the event of the employment contract being terminated within a specific number of years.

- differences in the conditions applying to pension funds;
- differences in the tax laws applying to the cross-border building up and transfer of pensions.

Another important aspect to be borne in mind is that there are many different types of cross-border situation. A distinction may have to be made, for example, between temporary emigration (secondment), permanent emigration and frontier employees. Separate arrangements may also need to be made for certain special groups. Of particular importance in this respect is the Draft Pensions Directive referred to earlier, which essentially seeks to remove any obstacles in this area. I would suggest that this also needs to be applied in conjunction with an optimal harmonisation of fiscal and social security legislation so as to create a single, uniform system. I refer in this context to the discussion of the various types of income in section 3 below. First, however, I will discuss the proposals presented in the Working Document, the Green Paper and the Draft Pensions Directive.

2.3.5 *The Working Document*

In 1992 the European Commission published a Working Document.[25] This document contains a number of proposals for improving the ways in which pensions built up and transferred in cross-border situations are treated from a tax perspective. The document is only of significance for migrant workers who are members of company pension schemes; there is, however, a further restriction in that the document ultimately only deals with seconded employees. My view is, however, that the nature of what is being discussed and the specific proposals made would not exclude the possibility of a wider scope. The conclusion is that efforts need to be made to establish a system whereby arrangements would be recognised by Member States in the sense that seconded employees could continue participating in pension schemes in their Member State of origin. The main purpose of recognising foreign pension arrangements is tax-driven, i.e. to ensure that premiums are deductible and claims are built up free of tax. The tax treatment should tie in with the treatment in the country in which the employee is temporarily resident (country of employment). Of course, this requirement could conceivably result in part of pension arrangements not being available for tax relief; that would be wrong, I believe. The requirement is not, however, illogical. After all, the temporary host country would in this case have to grant tax relief, whilst it would be known from the outset that this country would not be able to levy tax on the pension benefits ultimately disbursed.[26]

---

[25] The Working Document contains a number of informatory appendices, although some aspects of these may well be outdated by now. The appendices provide details of such things as the obstacles preventing migrant workers from joining pension schemes in their countries of origin and an overview of the various types of pension fund in the Member States in which the general tax treatment applied is of a similar nature.

[26] Unless, of course, the individual concerned were ultimately to become resident in that country. Even in the event of there being no treaty between the temporary country of employment and the country of residence the former could as such normally levy tax on

An argument against the structure presented in the Working Document is the fact that tax relief may be unavailable for part of a pension provision, whilst the benefits would in due course be taxed in full. In my view, this aspect presents a greater problem than the first issue discussed.

2.3.6 *The Green Paper*

In June 1997 the European Commission published the Green Paper *Supplementary Pensions in the Single Market.* This is often referred to as the Pensions Green Paper. There are two main reasons for wanting to devote more attention to the subject of legislation on supplementary pensions. First, the increasing international mobility of labour is having a substantial impact on the building up of pensions. In addition, the role of governments in state pension schemes is very likely to become more limited as a result of ageing populations. In order to remove as many obstacles as possible in this respect it is proposed that:

- accrued pension claims should not be lost as a result of emigration;
- cross-border disbursement of pension benefits should be possible without any restrictions;
- membership of a pension scheme in the original country should continue in the event of short-term work in another country.

The following objectives are important from a fiscal perspective:

- cross-border recognition of pension arrangements;
- no cross-border obstacles preventing tax relief on premiums, even in the event of the right to tax the benefits being assigned by treaty to another Member State.[27]

2.3.7 *The Draft Pensions Directive*

In November 1997 the European Commission published a Draft Pensions Directive.[28] This is mainly of importance for employees moving from one country to another, including those moving on a seconded basis. In this respect it anticipates the Green Paper discussed above. The essence of the Draft Pensions Directive with regard to the issue being discussed is as follows:

(Cont.)
the pension benefits. Nevertheless, it is not very likely that that country's legislation will provide for that since neither the employer nor the employee nor the entity disbursing the pension would have any links to that country, or at least not any more.

27 This effectively rejects the views expressed in the decisions in Case C-240/90 *Bachman* [1992] ECR 249 (28 January 1992, ECJ) and Case C-80/94 *Wielockx* [1995] (11 August 1995, ECJ), BNB 1995/319*.

28 Draft Pensions Directive of 19 November 1997, OJ 1997 C5. This draft became effective from 26 July 1998 by Directive of 29 June 1998, OJ 1998 C152. In the definitive Directive no fiscal facilities are required from the EC countries.

- accrued pension rights should be protected in the event of cross-border employment; no distinction should be made between voluntary and compulsory pension arrangements;
- each Member State should be required to specify which foreign pension arrangements would or could be eligible for tax relief in their specific country;
- individuals should be able to remain members of their original pension schemes in their countries of origin when seconded to another Member State on a temporary basis. In this case, temporary would mean a period of up to five years.

Although the Draft represents a significant improvement in terms of opportunities for building up pensions in cross-border situations and international transfer values, it certainly does not solve all the problems. In my view it is particularly important that the issue should be looked at more closely in conjunction with fiscal and social security legislation. A way in which this could be done is outlined below in section 3 and the following sections.

2.4 Concluding Remarks

In view of the fundamental differences between the various ways of implementing and the conditions applying to the three legislative areas discussed above, there is no likelihood of the rules on the demarcation of taxation powers, compulsory national insurance and pensions being harmonised in the foreseeable future. Neither is there much prospect of this in the longer term, in my opinion. Furthermore, there is no evidence to suggest that this is the aim of any of the efforts being undertaken, either at national, international or European level. Indeed, it is neither strictly necessary nor desirable. Nevertheless, current legislation does result in substantial differences, which in turn create a range of distortions and complex situations and rules. There is, therefore, much to be said for a greater harmonisation of the relevant rules and regulations, wherever possible.

I will now use a number of regularly occurring examples of the cross-border movement of persons in order to show what can and cannot be done. I will also examine ways in which and the extent to which these can be applied. I have based the discussion on tax and social security situations covered by treaty provisions, for example Regulation 1408/71. Any situations where either none or only one of the areas is covered by a treaty will be disregarded. In practice, therefore, the discussion will mainly be of situations involving European law.

3 Cross-Border Employment

There are essentially three main forms of cross-border employment:

1. an employee living in state A and working for a long, but not permanent period in state B (an ordinary employee);
2. an employee living in state A and working for a relatively short period of time in state B (a seconded employee);
3. an employee living in state A, working in state B and returning daily or at least once a week to state B (a frontier employee).

The capacity in which the activities are performed is also important. National legislation makes a distinction for payroll and income tax purposes between an 'ordinary' private employee, an employee in the transport sector, a director and a public service employee.[29]

Treaty legislation also distinguishes certain groups of employees, with these distinctions partly reflecting the different categories recognised in national law. The main categories are listed below:

Table 3 Categories of cross-border employees

Type of work:	*Assigned to:*
ordinary employee[30]	country of employment
seconded employee	country of residence
frontier employee	country of residence or employment[31]
director	company's country of establishment
public service employee[32]	source state/state paying employee's salary

The reasoning behind the assignment in the cases of frontier and seconded employees is largely based on the fact that the social and economic base of the said categories of employees is largely in the country of residence. Another important factor in the case of seconded employees is that it would be fairly impractical for the taxation powers to have to be transferred for a short period of time to a country in which an individual was working only

[29] See Income Tax Act 1964, Articles 48 and 50 and Wages and Salaries Tax Act 1964, Article 2 (3)-(5). A further subdivision can be made. Examples of other categories are sporting professionals, artists, diplomats and consular representatives, professors and university lecturers. There will be no further discussion of these categories in this presentation.

[30] Sometimes there are separate rules for employees in the transport sector or working on the Continental shelf.

[31] Depending on the treaty provisions; frontier employee regulations are not always included.

[32] A distinction is often made within the public service employees category for university professors working abroad on a temporary basis.

temporarily. I do not actually see any good reason (at least not any more) for assigning the taxation powers in the case of a director to the state in which the director's employer is located. The same applies to ordinary public service employees–at least certainly nowadays, when there is little if any meaningful difference between public and private sector employees. Both in respect of income earned by directors and by public service employees I would argue, therefore, in favour of abolishing the specific rules of assignment and simply subjecting the said income to the rules governing general earned income (OECD Model Convention, Article 15); the specific rules of assignment should, however, continue to apply to diplomats and consular representatives, given their special positions.[33] I will examine this issue in more detail when discussing the various different groups of persons.

In principle, the various types of employee referred to above are also 'recognisable' in international social security legislation. It is striking nevertheless that the categories of employees distinguished in international tax legislation are not quite the same as those recognised in social security legislation. Frontier employees[34] and directors, for example, are not treated as separate categories. On the other hand, other groups such as public service employees and transport employees are singled out. Interestingly, this further subdivision is only seen in national legislation, not at an international level. The tendency in international legislation is usually only to specify private sector employees and sometimes also public sector employees. This generally means that where the obligation for employees to be insured arises on the basis of international legislation, there is a great deal of uniformity. The fact that the same cannot be said in the case of national legislation means on the one hand that there may be substantial assigning differences between situations covered by treaties and situations where no treaties apply. It also means on the other hand that the effect of any international assigning rules may be nullified in certain cases by provisions in national legislation. I would, therefore, like to see the number of special rules incorporated in national legislation being as limited as possible.

4 Ordinary Employees

Ordinary employees–i.e. those not involved in any special or specific activities and not employed on specific terms and conditions–usually present relatively few problems in terms of the assignment of taxation and national insurance contributions; these are consistently assigned to the country in which the individual is working, irrespective of where the

---

[33] That is mandatory under the terms of the Vienna Conventions of 18 April 1961, Trb. 1962, 159 (diplomatic relations) and 24 April 1963, Trb. 1981, 143 (consular relations).

[34] Regulation 1408/71, Article 71 for example, does contain specific regulations on frontier employees, but these do not cover compulsory national insurance contributions. See Regulation 1408/71, Article 1(b) for the definition of a frontier employee.

individual lives and the employer is located. This is regulated clearly in national and international legislation, which are generally well aligned in this respect. On the whole, I see no need for any changes here.

In the case of pensions, however, the alignment of legislation is often far less than optimal. This is because the laws governing pension arrangements are usually those of the country in which the employer is located, whilst this employer is often located in a country other than that where the employee works and/or lives. This can then lead to the problem of there possibly being no tax relief available for a pension built up under the laws of the country of employment. There are three potential solutions to this problem:

1. Recognition of the pension arrangements by the country of employment. This would in effect mean that this country's rules would apply to employee premiums (i.e. tax-deductibility) and pension rights (i.e. exemption from tax);[35]
2. Foreign employers agreeing to establish pension arrangements according to the law of the country of employment. If there is also an employer in that country, that employer could also provide pension arrangements. If pension arrangements are established in the country of employment, it would also be desirable for any pension rights already built up elsewhere to be able to be transferred;[36]
3. Employees could arrange pensions for themselves in their country of employment and be reimbursed by their employers.

The third option is undoubtedly the least appealing, whilst the first two ultimately achieve the same objective, albeit in fundamentally different ways. From an operational perspective, too, there is little difference between these two alternatives.

---

35 Recognition of pension arrangements and the granting of tax relief on premiums paid are essentially two different matters, specifically in those cases where the tax relief is, for example, dependent on the pension fund or insurer's country of establishment.

36 In the case of the Netherlands it is possible under certain conditions pursuant to Pension and Savings Funds Act, Article 32 et seq. and Wages and Salaries Tax Act 1964, Article 19b(4) (specifically in relation to the accepting of employment abroad). See also the Decree of 26 May 1998, no. DB98/2028, V-N 1998/30.18 in which it is stated that in the event of a transfer other than in the aforementioned cases, the transfer value can be taxed pursuant to Article 15 of the Treaty (earned income) whilst the individual eligible for a pension is resident abroad (in the Treaty country). There are absolutely no grounds for this.

5 Seconded Employees

5.1 TAXATION

International secondments are very common.[37] It is not surprising, therefore, that there are special rules covering them, both in respect of taxation and social security. In the case of pensions legislation, there are, however, no special provisions for secondments. Dutch legislation does, however, provide for voluntary contributions to be paid in certain circumstances (see above). Exemptions from compulsory pensions contributions are mainly of importance in the case of employees seconded to the Netherlands. Voluntary contributions could be an option for Dutch employees seconded abroad; in most cases, however, compulsory pension contributions will be able to be continued since the employer is and will remain based in the Netherlands.

It is interesting that the fiscal criteria applying to secondments differ in almost all respects from the criteria applying to social security. The fiscal rules laid down in OECD Model Convention, Article 15(2) are very strict. In addition to a maximum seconded period of 183 days, the most important stipulation is that an employee's remuneration may not be charged to an employer in the country of employment. Not only are the conditions themselves strict, but they are usually also applied strictly. From the very start, this has led to discussions, both in the courts and in publications, as to how the period of 183 days should actually be measured and specifically how to account for days off and annual leave entitlement. In addition, the question has arisen, again both in publications[38] and in the courts,[39] as to how to deal with the criteria specified in the OECD Model Convention, Articles 15(2)(b) and 15(2)(c) (basically, the stipulation that remuneration should not be charged to the foreign employer). This latter issue has not yet been resolved. My view is that the said provision has been formulated too strictly and does not properly reflect the specific features of secondment. These are essentially the fact that secondment involves a person working for a relatively short period in another country. Given that it is known from the outset that the individual involved will be returning to his or her home country within a foreseeable period, it is obvious that his or her life will remain based in the country from which he or she was seconded. Another striking aspect is that the period specified for secondments in the OECD Model Convention has applied since 1963 (!) and has never been extended. The 183-day period obviously needs to be extended, given the way society has changed since 1963 and the fact that average secondments have now

[37] The question of when a secondment can be said to exist will be discussed later. I will be disregarding situations which could also be interpreted as the acceptance of employment abroad or the lending of staff.

[38] See P. Kavelaars, *Toewijzingsregels in het Europees sociaal-verzekeringsrecht*, (Deventer: Kluwer, 1992), pp. 281-282 and publications referred to therein. See also P.E. Roeloffs, 'De grensoverschrijdende dienstbetrekking in het Verdrag Nederland-Duitsland', *WFR* 1996/6188, 340-344.

[39] See, for example, Supreme Court, 19 June 1996, no 30-883, BNB 1996/369*.

become much longer than in the past. In this respect, therefore, it is strange that a rule designed to assist individuals working temporarily in the Netherlands actually incorporates a period of up to 120 months (the 35 per cent ruling); the *Nedeco* ruling may also be applied in certain circumstances involving temporary secondments from the Netherlands. It is remarkable that no maximum period is actually specified, only minimum periods! From that perspective, too, the period of 183 days should clearly be consigned to the history books.

With regard to the other two secondment conditions (i.e. those specified in subsections (b) and (c) of the Model Tax Treaty: see above), the following applies: in most cases the 'normal' employer will continue to pay an employee's salary, although that is obviously not absolutely necessary. I see no reason from the perspective of assigning taxation powers why it should make any difference which 'employer' actually pays the salary. Similarly, I do not consider it to be relevant whether or not the salary costs are passed on to the 'temporary' employer. Although this is understandable and even necessary[40] from a company perspective and for the purposes of determining taxable profits, it is of no importance for tax assignment purposes. I would also argue, therefore, for these conditions to be abolished.

5.2 Compulsory National Insurance

Social security legislation has always interpreted secondments much more liberally, at least at an international level. National (i.e. Dutch) legislation assumes relatively short secondment periods of up to six months. The secondments rule in Regulation 1408/71 and most of the social security treaties essentially assume a maximum period of one year, with this period usually being able to be extended to two years without any difficulty. In the first year of any such period, secondment is compulsory, whilst it is optional in the second year. Regulation 1408/71, Article 17 allows for secondments to be extended to up to five years. Although the main purpose of the provision is to provide scope for special situations, experience has shown that extensions of up to five years are normally possible without any major difficulties. The approach taken in social security legislation is clearly substantially different from that seen in tax legislation. Given the views I have outlined above, it will be obvious that the latter structure is without doubt the preferred option.

A second significant difference is that social security legislation does not restrict secondment periods to employees, but also covers other individuals. Regulation 1408/71[41] in particular provides scope for secondments of individuals working in other than paid employment. Most of these individuals will be self-employed, but there are also opportunities for those in forms of work other than paid employment. Secondment arrangements for the self-employed are in my view generally fairly

---

[40] This is simply a normal transfer pricing rule.

[41] This does not apply (or only rarely) to the other treaties.

pointless, simply because such individuals are very unlikely to choose to operate their businesses temporarily from another base. One advantage of the wider scope for secondments provided for in Regulation 1408/71 is, however, the fact that it applies both to those working in paid employment and to those in other forms of work. In effect, therefore, the opportunity for secondments is open to the whole of the working population. Frontier employees and directors can, therefore, also make use of it for tax purposes. Furthermore, as the decision in the *Van Poucke*[42] case shows, public service employees can also make use of the provisions of the secondment regulations.

A third difference relates to the other conditions applying to secondments. Quite simply, there are no other conditions stipulated in social security legislation. In other words, it is completely irrelevant who pays an individual's salary and who is charged for it. As I outlined above, when discussing taxation rules I consider this to be the correct approach.

The above leads me to conclude that the fiscal rules on secondments need to be revised and should preferably be harmonised with the corresponding rules and regulations laid down in social security legislation.

5.3 Pensions

Lastly, the issue of pensions needs examining. There are no regulations covering this issue at a European level, whilst national (i.e. Dutch) legislation contains no explicit provisions. If an employee is seconded to the Netherlands, pension arrangements will in principle have to be made, even if the employer is not based in the Netherlands. In such cases, an exemption will normally be granted pursuant to the Pension and Savings Funds Act, Article 29. From a fiscal perspective, that is also the best solution since the right to levy tax on income earned during a secondment will in principle remain with the country from which the individual has been seconded. Complications only arise in the case of secondments lasting longer than 183 days. This is because tax relief is not automatically available for pensions being built up abroad. It is only if the foreign pension arrangements are approved under the Wages and Salaries Tax Act 1964, Article 19d and if Article 19a(1)(c) of the same Act applies that exclusion from tax relief can be prevented. Where this is not possible, the alternative is a value transfer from one country to the other; whether or not that is possible will largely depend on the tax regime in the country from which the individual has been temporarily seconded.

If the secondment is from the Netherlands to another country, an individual will normally continue to build up pension rights in the Netherlands. Exemption from the obligation to make pension contributions in the country of temporary employment may have to be requested. Continuing to pay pension contributions in the Netherlands will not present any problems providing the secondment is for no longer than 183 days. In

---

[42] Case C-71/93, *Van Poucke* RSV 1994/193 (24 March 1994, ECJ).

the event of a longer secondment, the opportunity for tax relief may be lost, depending on the regulations in the country of temporary employment. It is of course possible to choose to stop paying pension contributions in the Netherlands and to join a pension scheme abroad, although the disadvantage of that is that the individual will lose certain pension rights; there will then be a second loss of pension when the individual subsequently returns to the Netherlands. An alternative would be to transfer the value of pension rights built up in the Netherlands to another country. The Wages and Salaries Tax Act 1964, Article 19b makes specific provision for this. In such circumstances, it would of course be desirable for the value of the pension, including any amounts built up abroad, to be able to be transferred back to the Netherlands at the end of the secondment. Lastly, it is conceivable that the full amount of the employee contributions could be converted into an employer premium and the employee's salary reduced correspondingly. In these circumstances, no complications ought to arise.[43]

It is obvious that there are or can be a range of pension-related problems in the event of a secondment. Most of these difficulties could be overcome if the secondment rules applied in social security legislation were to be adopted for both tax and pensions. The above should be taken as a plea in favour of such a step.

6 Frontier Employees[44]

A characteristic feature of frontier employees is that they regularly–often daily and sometimes weekly–travel to and from their country of residence and their country of employment. In that sense, they do not differ so much from seconded employees, except for the fact that they live in one country[45] and work in another. An essential difference is of course that seconded employees are working temporarily in another country, whilst frontier employees are in principle working in one country and living in another on a permanent basis. Generally speaking, frontier employees' lives are wholly based in their country of residence and it is largely in that country that they make use of a whole range of facilities. In contrast, they will make use of relatively few facilities in the country of employment. That is the main reason why a decision is sometimes made in an international tax context to

43 In certain cases of this type, the foreign tax authorities have been known to disallow deduction of the higher pension contributions from tax once the artificial nature of the construction was understood.

44 The more usual term 'frontier worker' is somewhat dated; a more contemporary term would be 'frontier employee'. Although this term is not yet widely used, I have chosen to use it throughout this presentation.

45 This parallel is obviously not completely true: in the case of a secondment for a longer period, the country of employment may well become an individual's country of residence. Nevertheless, the idea behind the secondment regulations is that in the longer term the social and economic life of a seconded employee will largely remain based in the original country of residence.

deviate from the normal rule and assign the right to levy tax to the country of residence. The OECD Model Convention does not actually make any specific provisions for this.[46] In itself, that is not so surprising since there are of course far more 'third countries' than 'border countries'. The absence of a general rule on frontier employees has resulted in there being a wide range of frontier employee regulations, in terms both of the criteria used to define a frontier employee and the definition of the border area. The Dutch-Belgian situation provides a clear example of this, with regulations on frontier employees largely working smoothly, whilst this is not so in the case of frontier employees in the Dutch-German border area. Strictly speaking, the UK can also be regarded as bordering on the Netherlands, but in this case there are no regulations on frontier employees.[47]

Although the above reasoning can in principle be applied–perhaps even more so–to social security and pensions, there are in fact scarcely any regulations on these subjects; almost the only exception is contained in Regulation 1408/71 and relates to the entitlement of frontier employees to certain benefits.[48] In my opinion, it would be preferable to assign the right to levy national insurance contributions to the country of residence rather than to the country of employment. Nevertheless, existing legislation subjects frontier employees to the same basic rule applying to all other employees and, as a result, contributions are payable in the country of employment. This means, therefore, that tax and national insurance systems are completely out of line with each other. I would suggest that both areas should be assigned to the country of residence;[49] this would also bring the systems into line with most of the frontier employee regulations contained in bilateral tax treaties.

Assigning the right to levy tax and national insurance contributions on frontier employees to the country of residence gives rise to the question as to which criteria should be used to determine whether or not frontier employee regulations should apply; the following three methods are the

---

46 In the notes to OECD Model Convention, Article 15 it is stated that the Treaty does not include any general rules on frontier employees, partly because of the great diversity and specific problems which can arise in this context.

47 This is less of a problem since it would be impractical to travel back and forth between the two countries on a daily basis. If, however, as is often the case, the week is used as the frame of reference, there is little need for frontier employee regulations to be included in this treaty. Nevertheless, there is another criterion–which is, incidentally, directly related to the above criterion–i.e. that frontier employee regulations can also be linked to the distance between the place of residence and the place of work; in the case of the said countries, this distance is relatively long. As a result, there is no need for frontier employee regulations in such cases.

48 Some bilateral treaties do contain regulations of this nature.

49 M.J.G.A.M. Weerepas, *Grensarbeider: de pioniers van de interne markt* (University of Maastricht, December 1996). After extensive, thorough research on the position of frontier employees the author does not come to an unequivocal conclusion: she puts forward three possible solutions, without opting in favour of any one of them. The Ministries of Finance and Social Affairs & Employment have since started investigating the problems of frontier employees, with the aim of finding a solution to the problems currently faced. See the letter from the State Secretary of Finance of 13 August 1997, no. AFP97/207, V-N 1997, 3131.

main ways used to establish whether or not an individual should be regarded as a frontier employee:

1. an employee returns to his country of residence at least once a week;
2. an employee returns to his country of residence at least once a week; the border areas in both the country of residence and country of employment are specified;
3. an employee returns to his country of residence at least once a week and both the place of residence and place of employment are within a certain specified distance from the border.

The first example is more or less what has been specified in the Dutch-German tax treaty of 16 June 1959, albeit that this treaty provides even greater scope thanks to the fact that it is not even necessary for an employee to return to his place of residence at least once a week. I view this approach as being too liberal–even if there were to be a requirement for employees to return weekly to their place of residence. After all, the frontier employee regulations represent an exception to the basic rule, and to me that implies that restricted application would be desirable. There is a danger, moreover, of the distinction between normal employment situations and those involving secondments becoming blurred. The second alternative is used by the Netherlands and Belgium in their bilateral tax treaty of 19 October 1970. The main objection to this method is essentially the unequal treatment of otherwise comparable situations: individuals travelling the same distance will in certain cases be regarded as frontier employees, whilst in other cases they will not.

The method used by the Netherlands and Belgium is not generally accepted internationally and it is, therefore, not my preferred option. That brings me to the third option, where the distance from the border is the determining factor. In principle, this is the most objective approach and, therefore, the most preferable. Nevertheless, there is a drawback. Say, for example, that a distance of 30 km from each side of the border is used as the criterion. The border area is, therefore, defined as being an area of 60 km across. As both the place of residence and the place of employment are required to be within the border area, someone living very close to the border but working, for example, at a place 35 km from the other side of the border would not be covered by the regulations. Similarly, there could be cases of individuals working close to the border in one country, but living outside the border area in the other country. If these types of situation are also to be covered, the cumulative conditions needing to be met for frontier employee regulations to apply would be as follows:

- the place of residence and/or place of work is/are within 30 km of the border;
- the distance in one direction between the place of residence and the place of work is no more than 60 km.

Selecting 30 as the number of kilometres from the border is, of course, an arbitrary choice.[50]

Either of the criteria outlined above would be a fair way of applying frontier employee regulations. The regulations should not, however, be restricted to employees, but should also apply to anyone fulfilling the said conditions; in other words, they should also apply to directors, public service employees and entrepreneurs or professional practitioners. I see no fundamental difference between these various categories in terms of the rationale behind frontier regulations. Therefore, the frontier persons regulations should prevail over the general rules on assignment. An individual meeting the requirements of both secondment and frontier employee regulations–i.e. a secondment within the border area–would not present any problem since in both cases the assignment of levying powers would be to the country of residence; for the sake of completeness, it could also be specified that the frontier persons regulations would then prevail.

Secondment outside an individual's country of employment in a case covered by frontier persons regulations would create a number of problems since on the one hand the individual would no longer meet the criteria for the frontier persons regulations, whilst on the other hand the secondment would not be from the country of residence, which would normally also be the country of employment. For information on such situations, see also the supplementary ruling in the frontier employee regulations for Belgium and the Netherlands. In my view, however, these regulations gloss too much over the difference between seconded activities outside the border area but within the same country of employment on the one hand and seconded activities outside the country of employment on the other.[51] Given the rationale behind the secondment regulations and the frontier persons regulations, the rule ought to be that secondments fulfilling the 183-day criterion and where remuneration is generally and will continue to be the responsibility of the employer in the border area do not contravene frontier persons regulations. One complication in this respect is the fact that countries with a common border can reach mutual agreement, but that any agreement reached does not seem automatically to extend to third countries where seconded activities are being performed. If this principle were to be achieved, it would have to be incorporated into the OECD Model Convention.

The above is essentially based on the fiscal regulations for frontier employees; that is hardly surprising since there are almost no such regulations for social security.[52] I see, however, no fundamental and/or practical reasons why such a system could not be applied to frontier persons for social security purposes; indeed, a country of residence system for social security would also be more attractive for frontier employees than the

---

50 And thus also the distance of 60 km.

51 Decree of 21 May 1992, IFZ92/715, BNB 1992/283.

52 See Regulation 1408/71, Article 71 for details of the limited frontier employee provisions.

current system. It would, however, require amendment of Regulation 1408/71 and the various social security treaties.

In the case of pension rights being built up it is normally so that the pension insurance is based on the legislation in the country where the activities are actually performed. There are a variety of reasons why it would be best in the case of frontier employees if the pensions regime in their country of residence were to apply; there would then be no problems involved in recognising the pension regime and tax relief would then be possible. The latter is of particular importance, given that frontier persons regulations currently assign taxation powers in full to the country of residence. Frontier employees will also normally continue to live in the same country of residence after retirement. That means, therefore, that in principle it should be straightforward to tax the pension benefits ultimately paid out. The main objection to such a system would come from employers, who would have to incorporate foreign pension arrangements into their administrative systems. The same applies, of course, to the tax and social security contributions that employers are required to withhold under the frontier employee regulations. To that extent, therefore, this objection is of only limited importance. If it is decided that this is not or cannot be the approach chosen, the alternative would have to be to apply the pensions legislation of the country in which the individual is working. If tax relief is to be available, the country of residence would have to recognise the pension arrangements of the country of employment and it would have to be possible for the cross-border pension contributions to be paid. Dutch tax legislation does not grant an exemption for pension rights in another country in such situations. The legislative systems in many other countries also will often not allow premiums to be deducted from tax in comparable situations. Provision could of course be made for this via the OECD Model Convention, but it would seem better in all respects for frontier employees to build up their pensions under the laws of their countries of residence.

7 Directors

7.1 Taxation

The director of an entity is only recognised as such in the treaties designed to prevent double taxation. Neither national legislation nor the social security system make a distinction between directors and other individuals. Case law on this subject shows that it is not possible to provide a simple definition of a director; the specific circumstances of the case in question and national civil law may both have to be taken into account.[53] Under Dutch tax legislation, a director is normally regarded as an employee, whether or not this reflects the actual situation. The same applies for

53 See, for example, Supreme Court, 26 August 1981, no. 20-413, BNB 1981/307* regarding those employees who are authorised to bind an entity, but who are not directors.

national insurance, with the exception of the employee contributions in the case of a director who is also a major shareholder. Legislation in other countries is in a number of cases different in this respect as directors may often be regarded as being self-employed. Lastly, pensions legislation does not recognise the concept of a director as such. In all such cases, therefore, the position of a director will have to be determined on the basis of the varying regulations in the different countries. This will, of course, often result in differing answers to the question of whether or not an individual should be categorised as a director and also differences in terms of which country is assigned the right to levy tax and national insurance contributions.

In view of the above, the question arises as to whether there are sufficient grounds for regarding directors as a separate case for the purposes of applying tax treaties. The main reason for doing this would seem to be that directors regularly perform services in a number of different countries and the periods involved are generally short.[54] It is not very practical, therefore, to assign taxation powers to a country that is only a country of employment on a temporary basis. Assigning the powers to tax income earned as a director to one specific country is certainly a better option from this perspective, and most of the existing treaties have chosen to assign to the company's country of residence. This will normally also be the country in which most of the director's work is done and the country of which he or she is a resident. I see no reasons of any substance for the assignment rules applying to directors to be different from those applying to ordinary employees. If there is indeed no reason for this distinction to be made, the question then arises as to whether a director should primarily be regarded as an employee or covered by the regulations applying to the self-employed or professional practitioners. It makes very little difference from the perspective of the primary assignment of levying powers since these are always assigned to the country of employment. It is certainly important, however, in the case of the special rules and regulations as there are secondment regulations and sometimes frontier persons regulations for employees that do not apply to the self-employed or professional practitioners and for which there is generally little need. Nevertheless, there are directors within the meaning of OECD Model Convention, Article 16 who are in positions differing very little from those of ordinary employees; board members are a good example of this. I believe that these individuals should be regarded as employees and covered by the relevant articles in legislation. There are, however, also directors and board members who are owners or part-owners of their company.[55] Depending on their stakeholdings, their positions are often comparable to those of self-employed entrepreneurs. I would argue that the second category of

---

[54] The following reasoning is given in the commentary to the OECD Model Convention (section 3): 'Since it might be sometimes difficult to ascertain where the services are performed, the provision treats the services as performed in the State of residence of the company'.

[55] In practical terms, this will involve ownership of shares.

individuals should be treated in the same way as the self-employed and professional practitioners in this respect, as they have been in the Netherlands since 1986 for the purposes of the employed persons insurance schemes, since 1997 for the purposes of the substantial shareholding regulations and since 1998 for the self-employed persons' invalidity insurance scheme (WAZ). That implies in effect that the position of a director/owner has to be examined on a case-by-case basis. So as to prevent the actual examination becoming too unwieldy, I would recommend using a quantitative criterion for the purposes of deciding which directors should be regarded as employees. For the reasons outlined above, I would tend to believe that voting rights should be the determining factor[56] and that the threshold should not be set too high. After all, entrepreneurship is also possible with a relatively small stake in a company.[57] A minimum threshold of 5-10 per cent of total voting rights could be set. For those covered by this assignment rule, there would be no need for special secondment regulations as the place where the main activities are performed would decide the country to which powers should be assigned. In the event of work being performed temporarily outside that country, the same country would retain levying powers. No account is taken in this respect of activities performed by frontier employees.[58]

The consequence for directors who are covered, on the basis of the above proposal, by OECD Model Convention, Article 15 will normally be that their earnings will be fully taxed in their country of work, which will also usually be the country in which the entity is resident; this is because when working for temporary periods outside their normal country of work/the company's country of residence, directors will in principle have recourse to secondment regulations. The important factor then, of course, will be whether and to what extent these will be able to be amended (see section 5.1 above for details). If the director is a frontier employee, he or she should also be able to be covered by any frontier employee regulations there may be, and in that case taxation powers will be assigned to the country of residence. In these types of situation, too, secondment regulations will be needed since it must be ensured that trips of short duration to third countries do not result in the taxation powers being transferred to those third countries or possibly to the country of employment.

7.2 Social Security

As mentioned earlier, social security legislation does not recognise directors as a separate category at either a national or international level. What is seen to some extent is a distinction being made between those directors most

56 See also, for example, the Merger Directive on this subject.

57 This is well-illustrated by fiscal case law on the subject of entrepreneurship and limited partners.

58 It is certainly conceivable that specific secondment regulations could also be available for this category of frontier employees. I will not be discussing this aspect in any more detail on this occasion.

comparable to ordinary employees and those who are more comparable to the self-employed. The general rule is that directors are regarded as employees and that, therefore, no special rules apply. Only in the event of a director also holding a substantial stake in a company, usually in the form of shares, will he or she no longer be regarded as an employee. The position as director is, therefore, irrelevant from a perspective of employee insurance contributions as there is no obligation to pay contributions. In contrast, the fact that the director has a shareholding is of no importance from a national insurance contributions perspective; there, only the formal position of director is relevant. Given that a director–irrespective of any shares which he or she may hold in the company–is almost always employed by the company of which he or she is a director, he or she will to that extent be regarded as an employee. As the decision in the *De Jaeck*[59] case shows, European law follows the definitions used by the Member States in their national legislation and there are, therefore, no complications in this area. A consequence of this approach is, however, that the term 'director' can never be defined uniformly for the purposes of applying Regulation 1408/71. This is rather unfortunate in my opinion since it means that decisions have to be taken on a case-by-case basis–in other words, for each Member State separately–on the exact position of the individual from a perspective of compulsory national insurance contributions. It is also somewhat remarkable that this approach has been chosen within the European Union. First because Regulation 1408/71 sets out to coordinate the social security systems within the European Union, which in my view ought to mean definitions also being coordinated.[60] Secondly, the decision in the *Asscher* case shows that, in respect of the application of Article 48 of the EC Treaty, the Court of Justice assumes a uniform definition of the term 'worker', with the Court of Justice opting explicitly for a test of materiality: in addition to the requirement for salary to be paid and work to be performed, there must be evidence of an actual relationship of authority. The criteria to be used to determine this, however, are not specified. Deciding to approach the issue of defining a worker/employee in this way also implies in my view a decision to opt for a coordinated approach. It would be inconceivable for the test of materiality to differ from country to country. If it has been decided to opt for a test of materiality in respect of the definition of the term 'worker' for the purposes of interpreting Article 48 of the EC Treaty, it would seem logical for this also to apply in other Articles covering the free movement of workers/employees. This is of particular importance in the case of Article 52 of the EC Treaty, which relates to the issue of social security. This Article also forms the basis–again for workers/employees–of Regulation 1408/71; it would be logical, therefore, to conclude that the decision in the *Asscher*

[59] Case C-340/94 *De Jaeck* (30 January 1997, ECJ) and Supreme Court, 2 July 1997, no. 29-332, BNB 1997/308c*-309*.

[60] It could be argued of course that this is what was achieved by the decision in the *De Jaeck* case as it was decided that the national social security legislation in each Member State would be the determining factor. I consider that, however, to be a very broad interpretation of the term 'coordination'.

case (Case C-107/94, BNB 1996/350c) should also be important in respect of the latter regulation. The decision in the *De Jaeck* case referred to above shows, however, that the Court of Justice has not gone along with this line of reasoning and has instead chosen its own way of interpreting the application of Regulation 1408/71. In my view, this approach does not accord with the interpretation of Article 52 of the EC Treaty as it is inconceivable that the term 'worker' should be defined in different ways in provisions relating specifically to the free movement of workers. The differences in interpreting the application of Article 48 et seq. of the EC Treaty on the one hand and Regulation 1408/71 on the other hand should most probably be attributed to the wide scope of the said Articles on the one hand–i.e. the free movement of workers–and, on the other hand, the limited scope of Regulation 1408/71, which sets out to coordinate Member States' social security systems. The existence of such differences in interpretation is not justified by the above line of reasoning.

My conclusions are, therefore, as follows:

- from a perspective of applying the EC Treaty, the definition of the term 'director' needs to be based on a uniform definition of the terms 'worker' (or 'employee') and 'self-employed';
- there are no sufficiently strong reasons for abandoning the idea of a uniform definition when implementing rules based on the EC Treaty (e.g. Regulation 1408/71);[61]
- assuming a uniform approach, I believe that tests of materiality should be applied to interpret the term 'worker' (or 'employee');
- in the case of directors, those without shareholdings or voting rights will, therefore, automatically be regarded as employees;
- for directors with voting rights or shareholdings, a test of materiality is needed. As in the case of taxation, this should take the form of a minimum threshold for voting rights or shareholdings.

I see no reason to apply any criterion other than that stated above; in other words, shareholdings/voting rights of around 5 per cent or 10 per cent will mean the individual being regarded as self-employed, whilst holdings/rights below this level will mean the individual being regarded as an employee. Those not meeting this criterion will be employees.

In this way, the fiscal treatment of employees and the self-employed essentially runs parallel to the way in which they are treated from a social security perspective. The harmonising approach outlined above need not prevent national legislative systems from applying their own criteria: if the obligation for national insurance contributions to be paid is assigned on the basis of the coordinated approach, it may be that no contributions are payable under national legislation because the said national legislation does not regard the individual as an employee (or, alternatively, as being self-

---

[61] The same should also apply in my view to, for example, Regulation 1612/68 on the free movement of employees.

employed). This accords both with general fiscal and social security thinking, which believes that the application of international law should not result in tax or premiums becoming compulsory if that would not be the case under national law, unless, in the case of social security, exemption from compulsory national insurance payments is the result of the place of residence being the criterion.[62] After all, the principle of strong effect goes against the idea of an individual being excluded from compulsory national insurance contributions solely on the basis of domicile.[63]

7.3 PENSIONS

In, for example, the European Commission's Working Document referred to above it is stated that one of the ways to achieve a greater harmonisation and streamlining of Member States' pensions legislation would be to follow the line taken in social security legislation; in other words, Regulation 1408/71. On that basis, the above could be applied directly to pensions in respect of employees (pension rights will be built up) and the self-employed (normally, no pension rights will be built up). Secondly, it would be a way of ensuring that the rights to levy taxation and national insurance and pension contributions would always be assigned to a single country. Here, too, actual pension arrangements and the rules governing them are of course completely dependent on the national legislation of the country concerned. Nominating Dutch pension legislation obviously cannot result in an automatic obligation to pay pension contributions in the Netherlands.

The important point with regard to directors is that the above proposals on tax and social security correspond more or less with the provisions of the Dutch Pension and Savings Funds Act. Pensions undertaken to be provided to employees–whether or not they are directors–either without any or with only modest shareholdings in the company may be treated differently from those provided to individuals with shareholdings above a certain level (Pension and Savings Funds Act, Article 2). The Pension and Savings Funds Act in effect sets out to make a material distinction between employees and non-employees and does that by stipulating a minimum shareholding of 10 per cent as the criterion. With regard to the protective effect of the Pension and Savings Funds Act (and, therefore, its application) a strictly formal criterion would seem to be being applied[64] as even an employee/sole shareholder to whom the company has undertaken to provide a pension is

---

62 See in respect of social security Case C-2/89 *Kits van Heijningen* [1990] ECR 1755 (3 May 1990, ECJ) and Case C-121/92 *Zinnecker* BNB 1994/203c*(13 October 1993, ECJ) continued at Supreme Court 23 February 1994, no. 26 403, BNB 1994/204*. For an exception to the said ruling in respect of the levying of taxation, see the decision in the frontier public servant case Supreme Court, 12 March 1980, no. 19-180, BNB 1980/170*.

63 See *Zinnecker* case referred to above.

64 This issue has been widely discussed: it can certainly be argued that the Pension and Savings Funds Act should not apply at all to self-administered pensions being built up. See in this respect: P.W. Roselle, 'Afkoopverbod dga (on)verbindend?', *WFR* 1996/6219, 1575-1588.

entitled to build up a pension protected by the Pension and Savings Funds Act; employment law provisions would seem to be the determining factor in this situation.

I am not wholly convinced that the above is the correct route. On the one hand, a formal criterion is used to determine who is entitled to receive a pension in due course, with the determining factor ultimately being the civil law employment contract. However, a material criterion is then used to determine the opportunities for building up a self-administered pension. Self-administration, as indicated above, can actually lead to the assumption that the whole of the Pension and Savings Funds Act will then not apply. For that reason, it would seem more correct to me–on the basis of the self-employed being neither entitled nor able to build up a pension–that the same should also apply to directors regarded as being self-employed entrepreneurs, i.e. those directors who also hold shares in the company. The obvious step then would be to apply the same criterion of 5-10 per cent of voting rights or shares. On a more fundamental point, I believe incidentally that the self-employed and these types of director/shareholder should generally have the opportunity to build up substantial retirement provisions; the pensions built up should be granted tax relief and be of a genuine nature. Those who should be regarded as directors in this sense can be determined on the basis of the above 5-10 per cent criterion.

8 Supervisory Board Directors

8.1 Taxation and Social Security

Supervisory Board directors are recognised as a separate category in tax legislation, but not in social security legislation. Such a director will be regarded as a fictitious employee[65] for payroll tax purposes; this will of course also apply for national insurance purposes. For the purposes of applying tax treaties, the individual will be covered by the regulations pertaining to directors; in other words, the right to levy tax on income earned as a Supervisory Board director will be assigned to the country in which the specific company is resident, regardless of where the Supervisory Board director's activities are actually performed. A similar approach is seen in Dutch payroll tax legislation (Wages and Salaries Tax Act 1964, Article 2(3)(c)) in respect of non-resident Supervisory Board directors of companies resident in the Netherlands. I will now go on to explain why I am not in favour of this. Supervisory Board directors are not relevant to the employed persons insurance schemes since it is assumed that these directors are not working on an employed basis. International social security regulations do not recognise Supervisory Board directors as a separate category. The question then arises as to whether or not these

[65] Wages and Salaries Tax Act 1964, Article 3(1)(h).

individuals should be regarded as employees or self-employed and whether or not the activities they perform are performed in or outside paid employment. In view of their role as independent advisors I would say that they could never be regarded as working on the basis of paid employment. Similarly, it would not be correct, I believe, for them to be regarded as self-employed. The decision in the *De Jaeck*[66] case should be able to provide clarification of this issue at a European level; both the ECJ and subsequently the SC ruled that the definition of an employee/self-employed individual and the issue of whether activities were deemed to be performed as part of or outside paid employment were matters for national social security legislation and this meant in the case of the director/major shareholder that the individual would be regarded as an employee. On this basis, therefore, the Supervisory Board director would then not be regarded as an employee. In my view it would also be incorrect to regard the individual as being self-employed; the correct approach would be to regard the Supervisory Board director as performing services other than in paid employment.[67] This situation is clearly the result of the fact that the social security treaties only make a distinction between the two categories of individuals within the working population, whilst the tax treaties make a further subdivision based on the types of activity performed. Although understandable,[68] this distinction is too restricted from a social security perspective. The significance of the distinction between employees and the self-employed is also limited since the country to which powers are assigned is the same in both cases.

The result of the above is that treaties assign taxation powers to the country in which the company is resident, whilst the right to levy social security premiums will normally be assigned to the country in which the actual activities are performed; this may of course also be the country in which the company is resident, but–and this is not at all unusual–if the Supervisory Board director performs some of the activities at home, i.e. in his or her country of residence, compulsory national insurance contributions will be payable in that country of residence. This will mean, therefore,

---

66 Case C-340/94 *De Jaeck* BNB 1997/308* (30 January 1997, ECJ) and Supreme Court, 2 July 1997, no. 29-332, BNB 1997/309*.

67 Some Supervisory Board directors have so many supervisory directorships that, if they were to be combined, they could constitute an enterprise. In certain circumstances the directors could be deemed to be self-employed entrepreneurs. In that context, it is interesting to note that Supervisory Board directors in the Netherlands are not covered by the Invalidity Insurance Act for Employed Persons (WAO), but are, therefore, covered by the Invalidity Insurance Act for the Self-Employed (WAZ), which only covers those not deemed to be employees. From that perspective, therefore, Supervisory Board directors are self-employed for the purposes of national social security legislation. Regulation 1408/71 is in line with that, as the decision in the *De Jaeck* case shows.

68 The explanation is simply that most countries make a distinction between social security legislation relating to employees on the one hand and that relating to the self-employed on the other. As far as I am aware, Supervisory Board directors are neither regarded as employees nor as being self-employed. The Dutch system of employed persons insurance schemes and national insurance schemes is unique in that respect.

that the tax on the income will be payable in one country and the social security premiums in another.

The question is whether or not the structure outlined above is the desired structure. The activities performed by such directors are by definition of a supervisory nature. This means that independence and autonomy are prerequisites. In this respect, the work of the Supervisory Board director is substantially different from that of other directors. The former's position is most comparable to that of a self-employed entrepreneur, who after all also operates independently. An important difference is, of course, the fact that the activities of the Supervisory Board director are of an incidental nature and to some extent are or can be performed at home. In practice, the activities will, therefore, only be performed to a limited degree in the country in which the company is resident; moreover, it is not an automatic requirement for the Supervisory Board meetings to be held in the country in which the company is resident, although shareholders' meetings will normally have to be held in that country. I conclude from this that the Supervisory Board director's links with the country in which the activities are performed and the country in which the company is resident are relatively weak in material terms, although he or she will of course have a formal relationship with the latter country. In view of these various aspects, my view is that in cross-border situations there are neither sufficiently strong links with the country in which the activities are performed nor with the country in which the company is resident for the right to levy tax and social security charges to be assigned to that country; it would, therefore, be best to assign the relevant powers to the director's country of residence. This approach would also reflect the reality that Supervisory Board directors often do or can perform some of their activities at home and that their social and economic ties are also usually mainly with their country of residence.

8.2 Pension Problems

There are a number of aspects which should be borne in mind in respect of the problems which can occur in the pensions sphere. Pension arrangements may be made for a Supervisory Board director, but these will not automatically be covered by the Pension and Savings Funds Act[69] since pension commitments within the meaning of the Pension and Savings Funds Act can only arise on the basis of a contract of employment (Pension and Savings Funds Act, Article 2)[70] and there is no such contract in the case of Supervisory Board directors. Given the Supervisory Board director's position, I would regard it as fairly illogical for him or her to be able to build up a pension since pension rights are typically a form of deferred salary

---

69 Taxation on pension arrangements may be on a deferred basis according to the taxation on disbursement rule ('*omkeerregel*'). In certain circumstances no account even has to be taken of the basic state retirement pension. See the publication in Infobulletin 88/11, V-N 1988, 398.

70 See Decree of 23 December 1996, Stb. 1997, 36 (Pension Commitments Decree).

from employment and, as outlined above, a specific feature of the Supervisory Board director's role is that it is not performed on the basis of an employment contract.

In view of the fact that a Supervisory Board director may build up a private law pension, it is important to ascertain whether or not tax relief will be available in such circumstances. Current legislation will not normally present any problems since any pension there may be will be undertaken to be provided by the company for which the director performs the supervisory activities, with the right to levy tax also being assigned to the country in which that company is resident. Problems could arise in respect of any tax relief that may be available on premiums paid since the obligation to pay contributions will be in the country in which the activities are actually performed. If some of these activities, as discussed above, are performed in the director's country of residence and some in the country in which the company is resident, the right to levy national insurance premiums will be assigned to the director's country of residence. And then, of course, the question arises as to whether tax relief will be available on the pension premiums paid; this will largely depend on whether the foreign pension arrangements are recognised in that country. This problem is comparable to that faced by ordinary employees.

As I indicated above, I am in favour of the right to levy tax and national insurance contributions on income earned as a Supervisory Board director being assigned to the director's country of residence. This approach should not present any obvious problems, assuming that the Supervisory Board director will not be building up pension rights. Any provisions or supplementary provisions made in this respect by the individual will, therefore, be in his or her private capacity. Tax relief would not present any particular problems in this respect. As it has normally been agreed that the right to tax pension benefits should also be assigned to the director's country of residence, this approach would also create a balanced structure from this perspective, too.

9 Public Service Employees

Both the tax and social security positions of the public service employees have been regulated at an international level. Most of these rules and regulations are in line with each other, and consequently there are few complications. In both areas, assignment is to the state employing the individual[71] and there are no discrepancies of any significance;[72] moreover,

---

71 OECD Model Convention, Article 19 and Regulation 1408/71, Article 13(2)(c). It is also stated consistently in national tax and social security legislation that assignment is to the state for which the public servant is working.

72 The specific position of public service employees has nevertheless led to a number of special decisions in the courts. In the *Van Poucke* case mentioned above, for example, it was decided in respect of the application of Regulation 1408/71, Article 14 that the public service employee should be treated in the same way as a private sector employee.

the pension is also built up in the state employing the individual. In view of this, there is little need to change the system of assignment applying in such cases. On the other hand, however, there are fewer and fewer reasons, both under Dutch law[73] and on the basis of international norms, for public service employees to be treated differently from their colleagues in the private sector. I believe, therefore, that the special status accorded to public service employees should be abolished, except where this would create other problems, for example in the case of diplomats and consular representatives[74] or individuals working for international or supranational organisations.[75] Incidentally, the treaties do not of course contain provisions covering such individuals since the organisations concerned are not linked in this respect to the country in which they are based.

10 Rights to Social Security Benefits

Social security benefits have only been regulated to a limited extent in tax treaties; where treaties contain provisions on levying powers, these are assigned to the source country. NSV and the UN Model Tax Treaty, Article 18 do include provisions to this effect. In the absence of such provisions, the other income article will apply and the powers will be assigned to the country of residence. In terms of the application of Regulation 1408/71, retired individuals will be insured in their country of residence unless the national legislation in the country paying the benefits specifies otherwise.

I will not go into this category in any more detail here since the issues involved are very similar to those involved in pensions, which will be discussed below. My view is that social security benefit systems should,

---

(Cont.)
From a fiscal legislation perspective, the decision in the frontier public servant case referred to earlier caused quite some commotion in the tax world since it was decided that a public service employee living abroad could, as a result of treaty provisions being applied, be in a worse position than provided for under national legislation.

73 Public servants still have a special position under Dutch law; nevertheless, there are certain changes in progress: the Public Servants Superannuation Fund (ABP) has been privatised (this does not mean, however, that the pensions themselves are now also a matter for private law as that is only possible in the event of the employer being in the private sector. See, for example, in this respect Supreme Court, 23 November 1994, no. 29-925, V-N 1994, p. 3914 on the commutation of a public servant's pension). Employment terms and conditions are now also increasingly being harmonised with those in the private sector, and within the very near future public service employees will be fully subject to the terms and conditions of the employed persons insurance schemes.

74 Their position is regulated in the two Vienna Conventions referred to earlier, in which the states commit themselves to various undertakings. One of the main purposes of these undertakings is to ensure that diplomats remain subject to the laws of the country for which they are working in order for their position to be influenced as little as possible by the country in which they are accredited. There is also reference made to this in subclause 4 of the OECD commentary.

75 Organisations such as these often have their own tax, social security and pension systems in order to prevent those working for the organisations from being treated differently depending on the country which they represent.

wherever possible, be in line with the systems applying to pensions, with the exception of temporary social security benefits such as sickness benefit. In those cases the prevailing rules of assignment should continue to apply. That indeed is what happens at present, both in tax[76] and social security legislation.[77]

11 Those Entitled to a Pension

This section looks at those who are entitled to receive retirement benefits in one form or another.[78] Tax legislation consistently assigns the right to levy tax to the individual's country of residence, even in the case of payments similar in nature to pensions;[79] the basic idea behind this is that the state provisions made use of by the individual entitled to a pension will all or almost all be in the country of residence and scarcely if at all in the country paying the pension. From that perspective, it is fair that the country of residence should be entitled to tax the benefits. In cases where the country paying the pension has granted tax relief on the pension whilst it was being built up there will, therefore, be a transfer of fiscal capital from the previous country of employment to the original/new country of residence.

At first sight, the system used in social security legislation would not appear to differ too greatly from that seen in tax legislation. Nevertheless, there are differences, with the most obvious being as follows:

- Fiscal rules of assignment vary depending on whether the pensions are governed by public or private law, whilst this distinction is not made at all in social security legislation. Given in any event the developments in the Netherlands in respect of public sector employees, I see no grounds for continuing to make a distinction between the two categories (see section 9 above)–nor, therefore, for it to be made in the case of pensions. The reasons given above for assigning taxation powers to the country of residence also apply, therefore, unreservedly in respect of public sector pensions.
- According to Regulation 1408/71 the national legislation of the country paying the pension should prevail.[80] Until mid-1991, Regulation 1408/71 still applied to retired people, but that was not

[76] See Decree of 8 October 1996, IFZ96/906M, V-N 1996, 4384.

[77] See Case C-302/84 *Ten Holder* [1986] ECR 1821 (12 June 1986, ECJ).

[78] These may, for example, be a transitional pension, an old-age pension or an early retirement pension. Surviving dependants and invalidity pensions are not included on the face of it; similarly, the following may not necessarily apply to these types of pension. Neither these types of benefits nor individuals' entitlement to benefits will be discussed here.

[79] A lump-sum payment, for example.

[80] Bilateral social security treaties hardly ever contain provisions relating to retired people.

the case with the rules of assignment in Part II of that Regulation.[81] Since then, the insurance obligation has been assigned to the country of residence pursuant to Regulation 1408/71, Article 13(1)(f) unless:

1. one of the other provisions of Regulation 1408/71 applies: in the event of the retired individual still being actively involved in economic activities, the latter provisions will prevail in respect of the rules of assignment;
2. the country paying the pension has specified in its national legislation that payment of a pension results in an individual being compulsorily insured in that country. In that case, national legislation will prevail.

The above means that assignment of the right to levy compulsory national insurance contributions on genuinely retired people has not been coordinated and that the pension assignment rules are meaningless in the case of those individuals entitled to a pension and still involved in income-generating activities.

- The same concept of pensions is used in tax legislation, although this concept itself is not actually defined. Normally, the way in which pensions are interpreted in the national legislation of the country of residence will be the determining factor. The fact that an 'equivalent provision' is included means that the concept has been stretched to cover other types of pension; transitional pensions and early retirement schemes are in principle also covered, as are lump-sum payments. My view on pension transfers and the renouncement of pensions is that these subjects should fall outside the scope of OECD Model Convention, Article 18. It is clear in the case of social security legislation that the above assignment rule has a much broader scope since there the nature of the benefits is not the determining factor. Instead, the only question of relevance is whether or not the individual entitled to the benefits is regarded as being retired. Retired individuals are those who have permanently ceased to participate in the labour market, either as an employee or on a self-employed or other basis.[82]

The conclusion, therefore, is that the social security rule has on the one hand a wider application than the tax rule since the nature of the benefits is irrelevant;[83] on the other hand, however, the provision only comes into play

---

[81] See decisions in Case C-140/88 *Noy* [1991] ECR 387, BNB 1991/40*, RSV* 1991/201* (21 February 1991, ECJ) and Case C-245/88 *Daalmeijer* [1991] ECR 555, RSV 1991/200 (21 February 1991, ECJ).

[82] See the decisions in the *Noy* and *Daalmeijer* cases referred to above. It was decided previously in the frequently mentioned *Ten Holder* case that anyone who is no longer working will remain insured in the previous country of work; this decision has been nullified by the decisions in the said cases in 1991. The decision in the *Ten Holder* case is still mainly of importance for those who have stopped working temporarily.

[83] The benefits may also be social security benefits.

in cases where income is no longer being earned from any form of economic activity.

I would be in favour of reducing the extent of the differences between the two approaches. This is not, however, a simple matter, as the differences outlined above indicate. There are also a number of other complications, for example:

- although most countries do grant tax relief on pensions being built up, there are some countries which do not.[84] That means that there is a conflict of interests between the two groups of countries: those countries which do grant tax relief will want to retain at least some of their rights to tax the benefits, whilst the other countries will attach far less importance to this aspect, but will instead emphasise the fact that those entitled to receive pensions will be making use of facilities in the country of residence and so should be obliged to pay contributions there;
- the extent to which social security charges are included in taxation under national legislation not only differs from country to country, far more than in the case of pensions, but also within individual countries in respect of the different types of social security. That makes a more coordinated approach considerably more difficult to achieve at present;
- the provisions of Regulation 1408/71 extend far further than simply the assigning of the right to levy compulsory national insurance contributions. The majority of the provisions relate to the harmonisation and granting of social security benefits. Account needs to be taken of these provisions when assigning the rights to levy compulsory contributions.

In view of what has been stated above, my initial conclusion is that the diversity of the basic assumptions and rules do not make it very easy to arrive at a harmonised model. There is, therefore, little point in seeking to achieve this. What is important is that there should be a certain degree of streamlining:

1. the right to levy compulsory social security contributions on retired people should only be assigned to the country of residence; the current exception to this rule, which involves the assignment of rights to the source country when stipulated by that country's national legislation, should cease to exist;
2. the right to tax all income earned by retired people subsequent to their retirement should (to the appropriate extent[85]) be assigned primarily to the country of residence, whilst the source country

[84] The exceptions are Germany (partial application of the basic rule) and Spain.
[85] This could be dependent on the extent of tax relief granted.

will be authorised to levy a withholding tax in the event of this country having granted tax relief on the post-retirement income.[86]

12 Self-Employed Individuals

12.1 TAXATION AND SOCIAL SECURITY

The self-employed are treated as a separate category both in tax and social security treaties, although that is not the case in all social security treaties. This is because certain countries have made no social security provisions for the self-employed[87] and there is then no reason to include provisions for the self-employed in a treaty. In tax matters, the rule is that taxation powers are assigned to the country where the activities of the self-employed individual are performed; this applies both in the case of activities performed within a company context (OECD Model Convention, Article 7)[88] and activities performed by a professional practitioner (OECD Model Convention, Article 14).[89] The right to levy compulsory national insurance contributions is also assigned to the country in which the activities are actually performed, regardless of whether there is a permanent establishment or base for the activities; it is interesting that Regulation 1408/71 also includes a provision to cover activities performed temporarily in another country (in effect, a form of secondment). This states that the obligation to pay contributions will remain in the original country of residence/work; the nature of the activities performed in a third country is of no relevance in this context.[90]

There is obviously a number of discrepancies between tax and social security legislation in respect of the self-employed. Essentially, these are as follows:

- income is only assigned for tax purposes to the country of work in the event of there being a permanent establishment or base there; this condition does not apply in social security legislation, where

[86] Here, too, there are various possible complications, e.g. if a pension built up over a certain period was built up in a third country which granted tax relief on the pension contributions and the rights and capital were subsequently transferred to the country which will ultimately be paying the pension. Such effects can be restricted, as the proposals discussed below indicate.

[87] Until recently, this was the case in the Netherlands. The Invalidity Insurance Act for the Self-Employed (WAZ), which came into effect at the beginning of 1998, has meant a number of changes in this respect. This scheme is designed to cover professional practitioners, who are in essence self-employed.

[88] Providing that there is a permanent establishment in the country of work; moreover, the right to levy tax only extends to income generated by the permanent establishment.

[89] Providing that there is a permanent base in the country of work; moreover, the source country's right to levy tax only extends to income attributed to the permanent base.

[90] Essentially, the only condition is that temporary activities (up to a maximum of five years) are being performed outside the normal country of work. During the first year the individual is compulsorily insured in the original country, whereas it is optional thereafter.

the 'only' requirement is for activities to be performed in the country;
- the assigning systems are completely at variance in cases where activities are performed in various different countries on a structural basis;
- in the event of activities being performed temporarily in a country other than the country of residence/work the decisive criterion from a tax perspective is whether or not there is a permanent establishment or base in that country. In contrast, secondment regulations will apply for social security purposes.

A good way of achieving greater harmonisation would be for secondment regulations similar to those applying in respect of social security to be included in tax legislation. This form of objective test would be relatively easy to implement and would avoid discussions about the existence or absence of permanent establishments etc. Another attractive aspect would be that the type of activities performed abroad would be of no relevance, whilst a further advantage would be that none of the profits generated in these circumstances would have to be attributed to the foreign enterprise.

12.2 Retirement Provisions

12.2.1 Pension allowance for the self-employed

In the Netherlands, retirement provisions specifically for the self-employed are limited. Other than the *Fiscale Oudedagsreserve* ('FOR'), the pension allowance for the self-employed, which is in effect simply a part of the business capital on which taxation is deferred to a later date, the only facilities available are the various pension arrangements which are compulsory in certain sectors. The FOR has no parallels in civil law and, from a fiscal perspective, is simply a way of deferring tax. The FOR can only be built up on the basis of profits generated in the Netherlands, whilst foreign tax residents are not allowed to build up a *FOR* under Dutch law. Following the decision in the *Wielockx* case,[91] however, this situation would appear to contravene European law. Surprisingly, the amendments to the FOR,[92] which came into force at the beginning of 1998, more or less ignored this aspect on the grounds that the effects of the decision in the *Wielockx* case had not yet been interpreted from a Dutch law perspective. Given the very clear way in which the ECJ framed its decision, there can in my opinion be absolutely no doubt as to what was meant. In this respect, therefore, it remains unclear whether and to what extent foreign tax residents not covered by the scope of European legislation can claim to be being discriminated against following the decision in the said case. My view is that there are sufficient grounds for demanding equal treatment, albeit that

---

91 Case C-80/94 *Wielockx* BNB 1995/319* (11 August 1995, ECJ).
92 Law enacted 18 December 1997, Stb. 736.

there will be hardly any individuals finding themselves in such a situation.[93] Given the specific nature of the FOR, there is no need for measures to be taken in this respect, although in view of what has been stated earlier it should also be made possible for the FOR to be able to be built up in cross-border situations.

The tax claim on the FOR has to be settled in the event of the self-employed person emigrating–irrespective of whether the business is continued in the Netherlands.[94] This is seen as a way of safeguarding the fiscal claim on capital built up under a FOR. The question arises as to whether this provision still has legal force subsequent to the decision in the *Wielockx* case. Strictly speaking, the decision did not relate to a case of emigration, but it would seem inconceivable that a self-employed person emigrating from the Netherlands whilst leaving behind and continuing to operate his Dutch business in the Netherlands would be treated differently from a foreigner with Dutch business operations. Furthermore, if the tax claim does have to be settled on emigration, the decision in the *Wielockx* case means that the individual can start building up a FOR again after he has emigrated. A situation involving emigration and the actual movement of persons would certainly seem to me to be covered by Community law.[95]

There are two possible approaches in the event of self-employed individuals emigrating whilst leaving behind business operations in the Netherlands:

- a restrictive interpretation of the decision in the *Wielockx* case: the FOR should be released and a new FOR built up after emigration. The funds released from the FOR can in any event be used to purchase an annuity, which will normally result in the benefits being taxed in due course in the country of residence. The FOR

---

93 In practice it is very difficult for a resident of a non-European Union Member State to operate a business in the Netherlands, except via a limited partnership. Following the amendments to the FOR scheme with effect from 1998, actual business operations are still needed if a self-employed individual is to build up a FOR reserve.

94 Income Tax Act 1964, Article 44f (1)(d).

95 The *Wielockx* case did not involve an issue of free movement. The party concerned lived in Belgium and had his business activities in the Netherlands. It would seem to me to be hard to defend the idea that where a situation is already covered by European law, emigration could lead to a reversal of this position. If this conclusion is correct, it could then also be claimed that Income Tax Act 1964, Article 16 (final settlement in the event of there no longer being any profits generated in the Netherlands) contravened European law (notwithstanding the decision by the Supreme Court, 27 August 1997, no. 32-333, V-N 1997, p. 3542, in which, incorrectly in my opinion, no preliminary questions were posed). In Belgium the Appeals Court would appear (Ghent, 28 January 1997, no. 1969/AR/29040, V-N 1997, p. 2765) to regard Income Tax Act 1964, Article 16 as contravening the EC Treaty. A crucial difference between Income Tax Act 1964, Article 16 and the continuation of the FOR in the event of emigration is that in the first case business activities are no longer being conducted in the Netherlands, whilst in the second case they are. In other words, a distinction needs to be made between emigration whilst continuing to perform business activities in the Netherlands and other types of emigration. Emigration of the business activities without emigration by the individual performing the activities will also result in tax becoming payable under the terms of

built up subsequently can in effect be accessed free of tax since the Income Tax Act 1964, Articles 48–49 do not actually make any provision for taxing withdrawals from the FOR. It is dubious whether or not the FOR can be converted into an annuity. A restrictive interpretation of the decision in the *Wielockx* case would seem to offer little scope for this. Moreover, there is no need for it since the funds will be released from the reserve free of tax;

- a less restrictive interpretation of the decision in the *Wielockx* case: this would mean that the FOR would not be released upon emigration and could continue to be built up or reduced after an individual's emigration. Withdrawals will not, however, be able to be taxed in the Netherlands. Similarly, there would be no need to be able to convert the FOR into an annuity.

12.2.2 *Compulsory occupational pension schemes*

Self-employed individuals who are members of occupational pension schemes do not face problems if they choose to emigrate. Claims which have been built up will remain effective, even if the individual moves the business activities abroad or ceases trading.[96] If the business activities are continued in the Netherlands after the individual's emigration, the question then arises as to whether the individual will still be able to deduct pension contributions from profits in the Netherlands. From the perspective of compulsory pension arrangements it will in any event be irrelevant whether or not the individual is resident in the Netherlands; similarly, the Income Tax Act 1964, Article 8(1)(f) also contains no restrictions in this respect. If the individual is resident in the Netherlands whilst conducting his business activities abroad, he will fall outside the scope of the Dutch pension arrangements.[97]

Benefits arising from compulsory occupational pension arrangements in the Netherlands are regarded as salary from previous employment, but are only taxable in the case of a non-resident if they are deemed to represent Dutch taxable income within the meaning of Income Tax Act 1964, Article 48. That is not the case; therefore, the Netherlands will never be able to tax income from these types of pension arrangement, irrespective of whether a double taxation treaty has been signed with the individual's current country of residence. An interesting aspect of this is that in the event of there being

---

(Cont.)
Income Tax Act 1964, Article 16; strangely enough, however, there seems to be no requirement for any FOR tax claims to be settled. It is not possible, however, to continue building up the FOR since essentially the only profits eligible are those regarded as having been generated in the Netherlands. Whether or not this restriction (also) contravenes Community law is open to question.

96 In such cases, pension rights will of course no longer continue to be built up.

97 A number of mandatory orders state specifically that the activities must be conducted in the Netherlands. Certain other regulations do not specify this. Given that the issue here is occupational schemes, which are by necessity nationally based, there would seem to be little scope for including foreign business activities in occupational arrangements.

such a treaty it is not actually clear how benefits should be categorised in view of the provisions of Wages and Salaries Tax Implementation Decree 1965, Article 11(2): the Netherlands regards such benefits as salary from previous employment, which ought to mean the Netherlands being assigned the right to levy tax; national legislation does not, however, provide for the levying powers to be effected. Were the categorisation instead to be based on the nature of the schemes, the pension article (article 10 of the OECD Model Tax Treaty) would obviously apply in treaty situations and the right to levy tax would then be assigned to the country of residence. It is interesting in this context that the provisions of Wages and Salaries Tax Act 1964, Article 11c do not actually apply to occupational pension schemes and that there are also no other comparable provisions applicable. It is, therefore, perfectly possible to opt for commutation or transfer of pensions to another country without penalty.

13 Conclusions

I am now coming to the end of my chapter. In it I have analysed existing international legislation on the demarcation and assignment of taxation powers and the right to levy compulsory social security and pension contributions in cross-border situations. I have discussed the various problems and distortions involved and also examined ways of achieving a better harmonisation of the various systems currently in operation. It is striking that each separate category has its own rules of assignment, but that there are no specific reasons to explain why they are as they are and they are all at variance with one another to a greater or lesser degree. This is only attributable, to a limited extent, to differences in the backgrounds of the various categories. In view of the rapidly increasing importance of cross-border work and the fact that such activities should not be obstructed I have looked into ways of achieving greater uniformity. My conclusion is that the problems involved in achieving greater uniformity in the assignment rules on tax, social security and pensions need not be insurmountable, particularly because the various rules of assignment currently in operation have been shown to lack any fundamental justification; similarly, there is little if any reason to apply the rules differently to the various categories of persons. On this basis, the most logical step would be to draw up a harmonised set of assignment rules for levying tax, social security and pension contributions, which would of course vary for different groups of individuals. I have put the case for this above, and I would support efforts to establish a single, uniform system.

Appendices

Appendix A: Supplementary Pensions in the Single Market. A Green Paper

Introduction and Executive Summary

The provision of pensions is a fundamental aspect of social protection in the European Union. This is made clear in the Commission's communication on Social Protection.[1] The present paper seeks to build on that communication by developing a number of ideas relating to certain aspects of supplementary pension provision. Currently there are 4 people of working age to support each pensioner in the EU. By 2040, there will be 2. This prediction is the result of greater longevity and the decline in birth rates in Europe. The average number of births per female in Europe has declined from 2.5 in 1965 to 1.8 in France and the UK to less than 1.5 in Germany, Italy and Spain. This phenomenon is not confined to the EU but is also found to a greater or lesser extent in most developed countries.

Statutory state pensions in the EU are mostly paid by the state out of current revenues ("pay as you go"). There are at present in general no earmarked investment funds for state pensions. If current policies towards pensions are not changed, there will be an inevitable increase in state spending on pensions to pay for the increased number of pensioners. At the moment state pensions account for 10% of GDP. Without changes in policy this will increase significantly by 2030. It will be difficult for Member States to meet these increased demands in view of the already high level of public spending in the EU and their commitment to budgetary rigour.

Several Member States have already initiated reforms to ensure the sustainability of state pension provision, and further reforms are being considered. Currently state pensions (pillar 1) account for the bulk of pension payouts (88%), but the need to maintain levels of income in retirement is likely to result in greater reliance being placed on the other

---

[1] Com (97)102.

main sources of supplementary retirement income:

- pension schemes linked to employment (pillar 2);
- pension schemes taken out by individuals, usually with life insurance companies (pillar 3).

The Commission clearly recognises that policies in relation to pillar 2 and 3 supplementary pension schemes discussed in this paper are by no means a panacea for the difficulties which demographic change is expected to raise. Member States' social security systems will continue to provide the bulk of pension payouts, with the emphasis on social solidarity within and between generations.

Consistent with the principle of subsidiarity, it is for Member States to decide on the role they wish each of these three sources of pension provision to play in providing retirement income. They can alter the balance between the sources directly, by changing the rules for state pensions or by making work-related schemes compulsory, or indirectly, through fiscal incentives. But given the existence and likely growth of funded supplementary schemes, the Green Paper explores how the Single Market can enable these schemes to operate more efficiently.

In contrast to state schemes, most pillar 2 and 3 schemes are funded: that is to say they are backed by assets which are invested to provide future pension payouts.[2] Even though the contribution of these schemes to total pension payout is currently relatively small, the funds invested to meet future pension liabilities are enormous: in 1993 there were 1 200 bn ECU invested on behalf of supplementary schemes; of the 1 600bn ECU of life insurance assets, a small but significant proportion represents pension provision.

They are likely to continue to grow in the future. Even if pillar 2 schemes in all Member States only grow to half the current coverage in the Netherlands and the UK (the Member States with the highest coverage at the moment), these funds would increase to 3 000 bn ECU.

The growth in these funds is one of the possible elements in maintaining the level of retirement income. They present an opportunity for the EU economy; the Green Paper asks how these benefits can be delivered through the EU capital market, particularly in the light of the positive impact of the introduction of Economic and Monetary Union. At present, employment and life assurance linked pension schemes in most Member States invest a large proportion of their assets in domestic government bonds. In view of the commitment of Member States to financial stability, it is likely that the capacity for growth in government bonds will be limited. This means that the supply of equities and private sector bonds is likely to grow if the increase in available funds is to be taken up by the EU capital market. The EU capital market will be transformed as a result, in particular, of the

---

[2] There are some exceptions for certain occupational schemes, for example in France where occupational schemes are pay as you go, and in Germany where pension provisions are backed by book reserves.

increase in the supply of long term capital. This could have beneficial effects on EU industry and infrastructure.

Some of the rules currently imposed by Member States as part of their prudential supervision of these funds seem to go beyond what is objectively necessary and prevent the freedom of movement of capital in the Single Market. Clearly, prudential supervision is required to ensure that pension funds and life assurance companies can meet their future pension liabilities. This supervision must not be weakened. One of the objectives of the Green Paper is to consider how the security of benefits can be maintained, removing the current disproportionate restrictions whilst allowing a real Single Market in pension funds to develop for the benefit of pensioners and future pensioners. From the evidence it seems that alternative methods of supervision can provide equivalent security. These alternative methods would have two additional advantages:

- they would be compatible with the free movement of capital and would encourage the expansion of the EU capital market. Such a market would be more liquid than individual national markets; and
- they would allow pension funds to invest a greater proportion of their assets in a variety of long term financial instruments such as equities, in line with the structure of their liabilities. This strategy could increase returns on the investments of pension funds because these instruments have generally carried a higher rate of return than government bonds.

The last point could be significant. It is possible that some EU pension funds could increase their current rate of return by diversifying and taking advantage of a Single Market for investment. Even a relatively modest increase in the rate of return over a typical working life could make a great difference to either the pension payout or the contribution necessary to finance a given pension. The lowering of the cost for companies of financing a given pension would have a positive impact on job creation. The Community is committed to improving employment in the Union. This commitment is borne out by the Commission's Confidence Pact and the employment strategy agreed at the Dublin European Council.

It should be clear that this Green Paper does not seek to endorse the investment by pension funds in equities or any other assets. It believes however that fund managers should be given the freedom to invest in the assets they consider the most appropriate for their particular pension fund and that this freedom should be exercised within a Single Market. This freedom cannot, of course, be absolute, but should be based on prudential rules and subject to supervision. The Commission is committed to ensuring that there is no reduction in the protection of pension funds. Prudential considerations are all the more important for equities given the greater volatility of these assets in the short term. The Commission is looking at alternative methods of supervision that are consistent with the Single Market.

This Green Paper also stresses the need to confirm the right of approved investment fund managers to offer their services in other Member States. This would not only give managers themselves the advantages of a Single Market, but the increased competition could be expected to reduce costs and encourage managers to improve their performance. The effect would be to increase the returns on investment, for the benefit of members of pension schemes.

Supporting the mobility of workers within the Union is a fundamental Community objective. Yet whilst arrangements relating to statutory pensions exist to facilitate free movement, there is no Community legislation on mobility in the context of supplementary schemes. Supplementary pension arrangements can pose a significant obstacle to labour mobility. This can be the case currently for moves within a Member State; the same is true, to an even greater extent, for moves to other Member States. The issue of migrant workers' supplementary pensions was considered in the report of the High Level Group on the freedom of movement of workers chaired by Mme Simone Veil, which concluded that action was needed to permit migrant workers to be treated on an equal footing with workers who move jobs within a Member State. This Green Paper considers the way forward.

Taxation plays an important role in pension provision and scheme design, providing privileged treatment at the level of contributions, fund income and capital gains, and benefit payments. There are regulations in place to control how these fiscal privileges are used. However, they can be an impediment to a Single Market, both for occupational and life assurance related arrangements, and can hinder the mobility of workers. The Green Paper therefore asks what initiatives are called for to make progress in this area.

The Commission believes the ideas discussed in this Green Paper can make a significant contribution to addressing the question of maintaining income in retirement and to reducing labour costs. Even if action must also be taken in other areas, in particular with regard to reform of state systems mobility of workers and taxation, the Union cannot afford to miss the opportunity that a change in policy towards the investment of pension and life assurance funds offers. This paper does not however attempt to deal with consumer protection issues (such as advice or mis-selling) except in the context of prudential regulation.

The Commission invites comments from the Member States, the European Parliament, the Economic and Social Committee, the Committee of the Regions, the social partners, economic operators, representative organisations, consumers and all other interested parties on the issues raised in this document. Responses to the paper are requested in writing no later than 31 December 1997, to:

The Director General - DG XV
European Commission
Rue de la Loi 200
B-1049 Brussels
Fax: (+32 2) 295 6500
Internet address: John.Mogg@dg15.cec.be

Chapter I: The Demographic and Economic Context

A. Current Demographic Trends

1. The demographic structure of the European Union is changing considerably. The dependency ratio (i.e. the ratio of the elderly to the population of working age) is increasing in most Member States and has already reached historically unprecedented levels. Over the last few decades two major demographic changes have taken place which lie behind the expected increase in the dependency ratio: a decline in the fertility rate and an increase in life expectancy. Although the long term effects of the ageing process on public budgets are rather uncertain and depend on the way the economy and society adapt to the process, there is likely to be significant pressure for an increase in public expenditure in the years ahead. Much of the pressure will fall on public social security pension schemes, which account for by far the most significant proportion of pensions in Europe, since expenditure on them is highly dependent on the age structure of the population. Similar demographic pressure is evident in the US and Japan.
2. The consequences of these changes are considerable. The combination of fewer births and longer life expectancy means that over time the ratio of those who have retired to those working will increase considerably. At present there are four people of working age to support each pensioner through social security contributions. By 2040 it is expected that on average those four people will have to support two pensioners. In some Member States the ratio will be even more unfavourable.

B. Budgetary Implications of Demographic Changes on State Pension Arrangements

3. The effects of these developments will be gradual. The Commission has conducted a survey of projections carried out in the Member States of future expenditure on state pensions over the coming decades.[3] The survey focuses on the most recent projections assuming current legislation, i.e. incorporating reforms already announced. The conclusions are as follows.[4]
   - *Over the period 1995-2030 as a whole,* the weighted average[5] of

---

[3] See D. Franco and T. Munzi, "Public Pension Expenditure Prospects in the European Union: A Survey of National Projections", *European Economy,* 1996, No. 3.

[4] National projections are not homogeneous in the coverage of pension expenditure. Comparable estimates of the impact of the pension expenditure on general government accounts have been produced on the basis of national expenditure trends and 1995 ratios of total public pension expenditure to GDP.

[5] Weighted by 1995 GDP in units of Purchasing Power Standard

pension expenditure to GDP ratios in the 11 Member States for which projections up to the year 2030 are available will increase by 3 percentage points (under favourable assumptions) and up to 4 percentage points (under unfavourable assumptions). Expenditure pressures will be relatively strong in several Member States which have not yet substantially reformed their pension systems (Belgium, Denmark, Ireland, Luxembourg, the Netherlands), but also in some Member States which have already introduced substantial reforms (Finland, France, Germany). Expenditure increases are expected to be fairly limited (under favourable economic scenarios) in Italy, Portugal, Spain, Sweden and in the United Kingdom.

- *By the year 2030,* in several Member States (Belgium, Finland, France, Germany, Italy, Luxembourg and the Netherlands) the ratio of pension expenditure to GDP may be in the range of 15% to 20%. Expenditure should be lower in Denmark, Spain, Sweden (in the 10% to 15% range), and in Ireland, Portugal and the United Kingdom (below 10%).[6]

4. At present, approximately 88% of all pensions paid in the EU are accounted for by state pensions. In turn, these pension costs represent a significant proportion of GDP – approximately 10%.[7] Therefore any increase in total pay-out on pensions by Member States will have an impact on budgets. Because of reforms already undertaken by most Member States, generally only *demographic trends* now contribute to the increase in pension expenditure as a proportion of GDP.

C. Current Structure of Pension Provision

5. In line with the principle of subsidiarity, it is for each Member State to decide on a national structure for pension provision that is in keeping with its particular needs. The relative importance of the three pillars in each Member State will therefore vary considerably, and will depend on the legal structure covering pension provision and the extent to which other factors come into play, such as the availability of tax relief. Equally, the nature of these pillars can be widely different. For example, in Finland, pillar 1 consists of the statutory state pension scheme and the statutory occupational pension scheme which is partially funded.[8] In France there is a very significant compulsory pillar 2, which is administered on a pay as you go basis. In the UK, there is a compulsory earnings

[6] The figures for Luxembourg and Portugal are based on projections to the period 2015-2020 only.

[7] Eurostat, 1995 estimate.

[8] Assets in 1996, 120% of the wage bill, 39.5% of GDP

related top up pillar 1[9] scheme, whilst pillar 2 arrangements are not compulsory at a national level. In Germany, Austria, Luxembourg and to a lesser extent Sweden, a significant proportion of supplementary pensions is provided through unfunded employers' book reserve schemes. In contrast, the setting up of book reserve schemes is no longer permitted in Spain.

6. Overall, employees in the EU rely for income provision in retirement on a number of sources. In broad economic terms, they can be described as follows [Table A].

Table A Income provision in retirement

Pillar 1	flat-rate, social security pensions (pay-as-you-go)
	earnings related, defined benefit (pay-as-you-go/funded)
Pillar 2	occupational pension schemes (pay-as-you-go/funded)
Pillar 3	life insurance based (predominantly) pension savings plans.[10]

The following table [Table B] shows the extent of the current reliance on pillar 1 schemes. By comparison pillar 2 schemes make up only 7% of total payments.

Table B EU wide pay out sources in % of total pay-out (1994–excluding Austria, Finland and Sweden)

Type of Scheme	
Pillar 1 PAYG,[11]	88.8%
Pillar 2 Funded, book reserve, insured plans	7%
Pillar 3 Personal pensions	0.9%
Other Means tested, guaranteed income scheme, poor relief programmes	3.3%

Source: EUROSTAT

7. *Pillar 1*

This is the basic state scheme, in which participation is generally compulsory. Schemes are financed on a pay as you go basis, where

[9] Subject to the possibility of opting out in favour of a private arrangement.

[10] This category is often seen as comprising any form of saving that might be used to provide retirement income, such as individual precautionary savings, residential property ownership, share ownership, family support, etc.

[11] Also includes the French second pillar, which is a pay as you go system with many of the characteristics of a state scheme.

current workers' contributions are used to fund the pension payments of retired people. These pension payments are guaranteed by the state, and the scheme is administered by a public institution. Pension benefits are calculated on the basis of a formula fixed in advance and are usually dependent on years of service. Pension income in retirement is usually indexed to inflation or to current wages. The link between contributions made during working life and benefits received after retirement changes substantially from system to system. Basic schemes in some Member States will provide for a pension which bears no relation to income during working life. In such systems there may be an earnings related pillar 1 scheme to top up pensions; contributions will depend on earnings, and benefits will be calculated by reference to those earnings.[12]

Advantages:

- Near universal coverage.
- Solidarity within and between generations.
- Alleviates poverty in old age and avoids for individuals some of the financial problems associated with longevity.
- Promotes social welfare.
- No discrimination for labour mobility, between jobs both within a Member State and between Member States.
- Insurance against inflation; avoids the consequences of investment risk.
- No selling costs.

Disadvantages:

- Vulnerable to the risk of population changes which can make current levels of benefit unsustainable.
- As pay as you go schemes have no underlying fund, they are vulnerable to rule changes. Governments may decide to change the basis on which benefits are calculated, thereby creating uncertainty about adequacy of benefits in the future.
- Where funding is through social charges, this can distort the labour market, through a perception of a tax on jobs.
- No scope for individual flexibility in the contribution cycle.

8. *Pillar 2*

Table I [see p. 126 below] shows the current situation of coverage of supplementary pillar 2 schemes. The variety of approaches in the Member States is illustrated by an example: in France the compulsory pillar 2 scheme is pay as you go and coverage is

---

[12] For example Finland, see paragraph 5 above

approximately 90% of those in private sector employment, making up 21% of all pension payments, whilst in Italy coverage of supplementary schemes is 5% of private sector workers and constitutes 2% of total pension payout. In the Netherlands, pillar 2 schemes account for almost a third of all pension payments.

Pension schemes in this category are generally linked to employment or the exercise of a profession (an 'occupational scheme' or 'industry wide scheme'). Membership of these schemes is limited to those working in particular sectors, industries, professions or companies, and will be created as a result of agreement between the social partners or by reference to, for example, standards in a particular industry. Pillar 2 schemes are administered by private institutions, and benefits are not guaranteed by the state. Contributions are set by reference to income, and payment of contributions is generally shared by employers and employees. With notable exceptions,[13] pillar 2 schemes are generally funded, with contributions accumulated and invested in order to provide benefits in the future, rather than to pay benefits to those who have already retired. The analysis in this section focuses on funded schemes. The link between contributions and benefits is closest in defined contribution schemes which provide benefits dependent solely on the return on assets invested. Returns on a member's slice of the fund will depend on investment choice, and ultimate pension benefits will depend on the value of the member's fund at the time of retirement. Funded defined benefit schemes, on the other hand, retain vestigial traces of solidarity, in that they allow for some redistribution of income among the members of the scheme. In defined benefit schemes the employer will effectively guarantee a level of benefits relating to the income of the employee at or near retirement.

Advantages

- Some link between contributions and future benefits in particular for defined contribution schemes, allowing workers to distinguish between contributions levied for pension provision and general taxation levied to pay for other welfare benefits.
- Largely resistant to demographic change.
- Defined contribution schemes: benefits linked directly to investment fund performance.
- Defined benefit schemes: employer's guarantee protects against falls in asset values. Some solidarity is also retained.
- Voluntary arrangements do not distort the labour market.

---

[13] For example in France, the compulsory ARRCO and AGIRC schemes; in Germany, the approach of many companies of backing pension promises with balance sheet reserves ('book reserves').

Disadvantages

- Coverage is not universal in all Member States.
- In some member States vesting periods (during which an employee will not have accumulated sufficient years of service in order to be entitled to a pension) are very long.
- Resistance to complete pooling of risks, so difficult to achieve equal treatment between men and women. (For example, if the pension is paid as a lump sum, this can lead to lower annual payments due to the greater longevity of women.)
- Defined benefit scheme: the approach to valuation of benefits of early leavers can discourage worker mobility between firms both within a Member State and between Member States (see Chapter V below). It can discriminate against those who take a career break. It has also been suggested that there could be a disincentive to employing older workers.
- Defined contribution scheme: investment risk is taken by the scheme member.
- Defined benefit scheme: where the employer provides a guarantee, the insolvency of the employer will remove that guarantee, making the scheme vulnerable to fluctuations in investment values (though the scheme is ring fenced and separate from the employer's own funds).
- Liabilities in salary linked defined benefit schemes depend on external factors such as inflation, and in particular, salary movements.
- Compulsory schemes may distort the labour market.
- No guarantee against the effects of inflation.
- Investment returns may not match expectations.

9. *Pillar 3*

Pillar 3 schemes may be used to supplement the first or second pillars, or both. They have many of the characteristics of defined contribution pillar 2 schemes, although participation is not related to employment or the exercise of a profession, and is arranged individually by contract directly with a product provider, generally a life assurance company. An individual's contributions are accumulated and invested, and the resulting fund in used subsequently to provide pension benefits for the individual.

Advantages

- If investment performance of the underlying assets is good, this can lead to improved pensions.
- Flexibility regarding contributions. It can accommodate career breaks and periods of part time work.
- Resistant to demographic change.
- Neutral regarding changing jobs.

- If the scheme is a life assurance pension policy, the policy-holder will be able in principle to benefit from the freedom of provision of services under the Third Life Assurance Directive, and so select an arrangement from a provider established in any Member State. However, regulatory and tax aspects, which may have an impact, are considered in Chapters IV and V.

Disadvantages

- Investment returns may not match expectations.
- No guarantee against the effects of inflation.
- No solidarity between and within generations.
- Cost: selling costs are generally high compared with first and pillar 2 schemes.
- Success depends in part on tax breaks.
- Risk of individuals' being sold inappropriate products.

10. *Group schemes*

Life assurance providers play an important role in pension provision. This can be through personal pensions, as described above. Equally, life assurers can provide management of group pension funds on behalf of pension scheme trustees. Such an arrangement falls under the pillar 2. A further option is for the scheme trustees to ask a life assurer to administer the scheme on the basis of a group arrangement. This is a "group scheme", and also comes within the pillar 2. Yet another variation is the group personal pension scheme, which, though organised through an employer, is a collection of individual personal pension policies.[14]

11. *Recent Member State reforms*

Several Member States have in the last decade or so introduced reforms to reduce the impact of demographic change on public pension provision. These reforms have been achieved in a variety of ways. In order to try to maintain the level of benefits, certain Member States have implemented an increase in social security contributions. However, given the already high contribution rates in most Member States, containment of spending is likely to be the primary instrument used to guarantee sustainability. There have already been steps towards decreasing benefits. Such steps include changing benefit indexation formulae, e.g. from a link with earnings to one with prices; increasing the retirement age and thereby the years during which contributions are paid, and reducing the number of years during which a pension will be receivable; reducing the proportion that pension benefits bear to

[14] The issue of group arrangements is discussed in Chapter IV.

income during working life (the replacement rate); calculating earnings related benefits on earnings over a long period rather than on the final year's earnings; reducing incentives to early retirement.

12. A different approach is for a funded state scheme to be developed to run parallel to the state pay as you go scheme. In Sweden statutory pension contributions are paid currently to the pay as you go scheme; however, once new legislation is implemented 2% will have to be paid into a statutory funded scheme. A more substantial systemic reform in the financing of public pension schemes would be a transformation from pay as you go to funding. Although this has been widely discussed, there are difficulties in implementing it in the case of developed and mature public pension systems such as those prevailing in the EU, not least the crystallising of future liabilities already 'bought' by non retired workers. This issue is discussed in the Commission's Communication on improving social protection in Europe.[15]
13. One option that is being considered, and indeed the process has already begun, is that Member States might gradually introduce conditions which are more conducive to the development of private funded supplementary schemes. The level of contributions is nevertheless unlikely to fall dramatically because; not only will it be necessary to pay the pensions of those already in retirement, but the role of state pay as you go systems will remain a fundamental part of the social structure of the Union. Private funded schemes are well established in several Member States including the UK, the Netherlands, Denmark and Ireland. Recent legislation in other states, such as Italy and most recently France, provides an opportunity for further developments in this area.
14. In essence, increased reliance on second and third pillar funded schemes would imply a partial shift in responsibility for retirement income provision from governments towards employers and employees, and towards individuals. Economic considerations point to the desirability of pension systems (the combination of both state and supplementary) which incorporate both pay as you go and funded elements, as these are subject to different risks and returns. However, as the importance of supplementary pensions increases as a percentage of total retirement income, it will be increasingly important for governments to provide a secure environment for the efficient operation of supplementary funded schemes. The role that the Single Market can play is explored in the next chapter.

[15] COM(97) 102.

D. CONCLUSION

15. Demographic changes in all Member States have prompted consideration of their effect on the funding of state pension schemes. Continued reductions in benefits and restrictions in pension eligibility to help to ensure the viability of public, pay as you go, schemes is one option many Member States are already implementing, though there are further steps to take. But this will have a negative impact on total retirement income levels. For this reason the trend towards the development of funded second and third pillar schemes is expected to continue.

It must be clear however that the development of funded schemes in the EU will not of itself provide a solution to the current problems of pay as you go systems. The sustainability of these schemes can only be achieved through further internal reforms. Funded schemes can facilitate the reform of pay as you go systems by offering benefits that compensate for a reduction in benefits from pay as you go schemes.

Chapter II: Retirement Provision and EU Capital Markets

A. Size of EU Pension Funds

16. The total assets in the EU of pillar 2 pension funds amount to 1.198bn ECU, of which the UK accounts for the largest share (717bn ECU or 65% of total) (Table II [see p. 127 below]). In fact, the two Member States with the biggest funds, the UK and the Netherlands (261bn ECU), together account for 89% of total assets of EU pension funds. The pension funds of other Member States are relatively small in comparison. This is a reflection of the fact that they are either not funded, pay as you go or based on book reserves, or have a very low coverage (see Table I [see p. 126 below]). The importance of UK and Netherlands funded schemes is reflected again when they are expressed as a percentage of national GDP (79% and 88% respectively), with other Member States falling well below this figure. The EU average is 20 % of GDP. For comparison, US pillar 2 pension funds total 3 546bn ECU (60% of GDP) and Japan 1 800bn ECU (45% of GDP).
17. The total assets of EU life insurance companies are nearly 50% higher than pillar 2 pension funds – 1 600bn ECU (Table III [see p. 128 below]). This figure includes pillar 3 pension policies but is made up principally of all life insurance savings schemes (that are not specifically designed for providing a pension) and life cover without a savings element (e.g. linked to a mortgage). Again the UK has the biggest funds (564bn ECU – 67 % of GDP) followed by Germany (380bn ECU – 21 % of GDP), France (317bn ECU – 30 % of GDP) and the Netherlands (138bn ECU – 46 % of GDP). The tax incentives given by each Member State are a factor in determining the size and growth of these funds.
18. Predictions of the likely growth of pension funds and pension related life assurance funds are difficult. Much will depend on the rules obliging employers to provide cover (pillar 2) and on the encouragement given through tax breaks (pillars 2 and 3). At the moment pillar 2 schemes cover 22% of the EU working population and only account for 7% of total pensions paid to those covered by such schemes. Even if pillar 2 schemes in all Member States only grow to half the coverage of the Netherlands and UK (the Member States with currently the highest coverage but still growing) these funds will increase to 3000 bn ECU. If they grow to have the same coverage as the Netherlands and UK they will reach 5000 bn ECU. Similarly, given a favourable tax environment, the funds of pillar 3 schemes could also grow rapidly as more people decide to increase their reliance on individual pension schemes.

B. How EU Pension and Life Insurance Funds are Invested

19. Pension funds and life insurance companies make investments in

order to meet future obligations. The pattern of investment varies considerably between Member States. The UK and, to a lesser extent, Ireland stand out because of the high percentage of assets in equities (80% and 55% respectively, which compares to the US with 52%) and low percentage of bonds (see Table IV [see p. 129 below]). However, funds in most other Member States rely much more on fixed income securities, mainly government bonds (e.g. 75% in Germany, 67% in France), and much less on equities (11% and 14% respectively). In all Member States real estate investments and short term placements are relatively small. The patterns of foreign to domestic assets also vary considerably. Most Member States' funds invest less than 10% in foreign assets. The UK and the Netherlands stand out, with 30% and 25% of their assets being non-domestic.

20. The pattern of actual investment for the assets of life insurance companies is similar to that of pillar 2 pension funds (see Table V [see p. 130 below]). Most assets are in fact held in domestic fixed income securities (mostly government) (e.g. Germany 75% of total, France and Italy 70%). Assets held in equities are much less important (e.g. Germany 5%, France 18% and Netherlands 12%). The UK is an exception with nearly 50% in domestic and over 10% in foreign equities. The reliance on fixed income securities in the UK is much less (25% of total).

C. Returns on Pension Fund Assets

21. Many studies show that over the longer term equities have tended to have a higher rate of return than bonds (see Table VI [see p. 131 to 133 below]), though this is not inevitable for the future. The investment strategy of a pension fund or life insurance company and the portfolio balance between equities, bonds, real estate and short term placements are principal determinants of the rate of return on overall assets. Because of the greater volatility of equities, any figures on rates of return are sensitive to the period over which these returns are measured. In the short term, therefore, equities could be outperformed by bonds, or could go down in value. Nevertheless, it is believed by some observers that because of the higher returns associated with equities over a long period, and because pension funds require investment over the long term, there is scope to increase the rate of return on some EU pension and life assurance funds, which currently hold a high proportion of government bonds, by increasing the share of equities in their investment portfolio.

22. It is difficult to get unequivocal evidence on this potential for higher equity holdings to increase returns. Any period selected is arbitrary. However over the period 1984-93 (Table VII [see p. 133 below]) pension funds in the UK and Ireland, with important equity holdings, had high real rates of return (10.2% and 10.3% respectively). Member States with around a third of their assets in

equities had lower real rates of return (Sweden 8.1%, the Netherlands 7.7%, Belgium 8.8%). The Member States with the lowest proportion of equities in their investment portfolio and a high percentage of government bonds had the lowest returns (Germany 7.1%, Spain 7.0% and Denmark 6.3%, the latter partly as a result of the tax on real interest rate). Other sources over other periods do not however give such clear results.

D. Impact of Differences in Rate of Return

23. The previous section showed significant differences in the real rate of return of EU pension funds and life insurance funds – with over 6 percentage points difference over the period 1984-1993 between the worst and best performers. In a funded scheme, returns need to be sufficient to deal with the effects of salary inflation over the long term. An increase in the annual rate of return of say 2 or 3 percentage points can make an enormous difference over a working life and should not be underestimated.

Assume the target is a fixed supplementary pension of 35% of salary on the basis of a 40 year working life. If the real rate of return on assets is 6%, the cost is 5% of salary: all other things being equal, if the real rate of return is 4%, the cost is 10% of salary, and if the real state of return is only 2% the cost is 19% of salary. Low rates of return on pension funds and life insurance assets will therefore mean:

- either much higher contributions from employers and employees: this will affect the indirect costs of labour, and therefore have an adverse impact on the EU's job creation ability;
- or much lower pensions for the same contributions and therefore more pressure on government spending in pillar 1.

It should be stressed that the Commission is not advocating any particular investment strategy for pension funds. It is the role of the fund managers to determine the best investment strategy for the ultimate benefit of pensioners, subject only to appropriate prudential supervision. This Green Paper is exploring the role the Single Market can play in the future to maximise the investment possibilities of fund managers whilst maintaining adequate prudential control. It discusses whether the current rules of prudential supervision in some Member States are disproportionate in that they go beyond what is objectively necessary to ensure the security of funds, and at the same time prevent the development of a real Single Market in pension funds for the benefit of pensioners and future pensioners (see Chapter III). First, however, it examines some of the asset management and supervisory techniques that are consistent with a Single Market in pension funds.

E. Can Higher Returns be Achieved Without Undue Risk?

24. Because their liabilities are long term, pension and life assurance funds can afford to take advantage of the generally higher returns offered in equities and long term placements. However, it is recognised that equities entail a higher risk than bonds, especially government bonds, and that long term bonds present a greater risk than short term bonds.[16]
25. Clearly, it would be unwise to pursue only high rates of return without any concern for the risk involved. Many of the regulations in the Member States focus on prudential controls designed to reduce risks to which funds are susceptible.
26. Advocates of modern risk management techniques suggest that such techniques allow managers to control risk while investing in assets with greater volatility but higher rates of return. These techniques aim to capture the return from the risk premium of equity while avoiding excessively high levels of volatility. In evaluating risk and making asset allocation decisions, it is more appropriate to focus on the relationship between assets and liabilities, and not solely on assets. For example funds would tend to make assets progressively liquid to match the date the liability is due – this avoids the effects of last minute bear markets or interest rates rises. Thus different pension funds (e.g. young schemes with many contributions relative to pay-out, or old schemes with large pay-outs relative to contributions) should in all likelihood adopt different investment strategies because their asset/liability profiles are different. In this way they can maximise returns at minimum increased risk.
27. In essence, asset/liability management (ALM) seeks to concentrate portfolios on long term assets with the highest returns, compensating for the increase of risk by pooling across assets whose returns are imperfectly correlated (diversification). Thus one asset with a high return but which is risky (i.e. volatile) may be offset by another high return but risky asset, if these risks are not positively correlated.
28. It is argued that diversifying assets is in fact a prudent approach, because over concentration in any one asset can increase risk and reduce rates of return. Even government bonds can fluctuate with changes in interest rates and inflation expectations. Consequently,

---

[16] For our purpose we can identify two types of risk:

- credit risk: the risk that the creditor will not pay because the company goes bankrupt or the government defaults. Over the long term these are reflected in the average rate of return of the different assets. Although of course in any one year they can be important and be reflected in the volatility of the asset.
- market risk: the risk that the price of an asset will fall such that the investor may not be able to meet his liabilities in that year without liquidating a higher proportion of his assets than expected. This market risk is reflected in the volatility of an asset.

over concentration of a portfolio on assets such as government bonds, that are regarded as "safe", can actually increase risk in comparison to a diversified portfolio, without obtaining higher returns.[17] Investment in a selection of imperfectly correlated markets will provide managers with a spread of diversified investments, and reduce potentially the risk of over concentration in assets denominated in one currency. One commentator concludes:

> Restrictions imposing arbitrary limits on asset holdings by type of asset, country or currency distribution run contrary to the prudential principle because they severely limit risk diversification. This constraint forces pension funds to assume more risks, while sacrificing return, and to conduct investment policies that are detrimental to their members in the long run.[18]

29. This approach to asset/liability management is the basis of the "prudent man" management and supervisory technique used in some Member States. They judge the financial viability of the pension fund or life insurance company by assessing the match between its financial assets and its liabilities over the expected life of the scheme, taking into account relevant considerations such as the type, size, development and rate of funding of the scheme, and the volume and nature of the fund's liabilities. When applying such asset/liability management principles, managers will also work within any investment principles imposed by, for example, the trustees or board. It is not a laisser faire supervision. On the contrary, it imposes on supervisors the obligation to ensure that the respective roles of manager and trustee/custodian/depositary are fulfilled in such a way as to ensure, in turn, that scheme members' benefits are secure.
30. The role of the supervisory authorities would need to be more dynamic if a qualitative approach to the investment of pension fund assets were to be pursued. Quantitative yardsticks would be much less prominent. When examining the financial health of a fund, supervisors would focus separately on its short and long term liabilities and on its investment horizon, the rate of funding in relation to liabilities and the need for the particular liability structure to be matched with an appropriate asset structure through an acceptable asset/liability management approach.

---

[17] See also Table VII [see p. 133 below] where some of the real returns on government bonds were negative over quite long periods.

[18] Prof. B. Solnik, "Fundamental considerations in cross-border investment: the European view". The research foundation of the Institute of Chartered Financial Analysts, April 1994.

F. How Could EU Capital Markets Absorb Future Increases in EU Pension Funds and Life Insurance Investments?

31. The development of funded supplementary schemes in the EU will increase the amount of financial assets available for investment. This growth will be very significant, but gradual. This section explores what advantages the creation of a real Single Market could have in increasing liquidity and reducing costs for pension funds. It also examines the structural changes in EU capital markets likely to come about as a result of increased investment by pension funds.
32. The supply of government bonds is unlikely to match the growth in financial assets of pension funds.

    Other vehicles for investment include principally equities and corporate bonds. These can be expected to play a greater role in the EU capital market in the future. In the US market capitalisation is much greater in relation to GDP (US: 68%; EU: 32%) (see Table VIII [see p. 134 below]) and the increase over time in pension fund assets has been successfully taken up by capital markets to provide adequate pensions.

    Because EU pension funds will have to find new investment outlets, private sector equity could, gradually, become one of the likely outlets for many funds. However the privatisation of state owned enterprises is likely to represent a relatively small proportion of the market as a whole. In addition, EASDAQ and stock markets for small company shares in a number of Member States could supplement conventional issues of equity available for pension and life insurance fund investment. Other new equity might also be issued by EU firms replacing to some extent the traditional sources of corporate finance in Europe.

    An additional area for development in the EU, as an alternative in appropriate circumstances to equities, is the corporate bond market. The market for corporate bonds is underdeveloped in the EU by comparison with the US, where the market is more than 7 times larger. If the US experience is mirrored in the EU, it may be expected that the market for corporate bonds will increase markedly in size.
33. Capital markets will adapt to take up these funds. Some of this capital may go outside the EU, though normal asset management practices would result in most of these remaining inside the EU.[19] However if Member States' capital markets are kept separate, they will be less liquid and be less able to take up successfully these funds. Therefore barriers to flows of capital which are not

[19] In the United States pension fund managers are not subject to quantitative investment restrictions. Because they have continent-wide opportunities to buy dollar assets, only 10% of their investments are in fact outside the USA.

objectively justified on prudential grounds, will reduce the efficiency of this process. The Investment Services Directive[20] has already removed many of the barriers to the functioning of EU capital markets. In addition stage 3 of Economic and Monetary Union will help this process by eliminating exchange risks for investors investing in securities issued in the currencies of participating Member States. Other obstacles, such as transaction costs and delays in implementing investment decisions, will also be reduced by a single currency, and should contribute to increased investment activity. Chapter III examines remaining prudential rules, applied by Member States, that are an impediment to freedom of capital flows and asks whether they are objectively justified.

34. Competition between financial institutions and between financial centres in the EU, together with the growth in financial assets available for investment, will lead to improvements in the EU capital market by reducing costs and increasing liquidity. This will be reinforced by EMU, which provides the opportunity for further development of an EU-wide capital market.

Question: The Commission seeks views on the analysis in this chapter.

[20] Investment Services Directive 93/22/EEC.

Chapter III: Appropriate prudential rules for a Single Market

A. Role of Supervision of Pension and Life Insurance Funds and Fund Managers

35. It is clear that pension and life insurance funds and the managers of these funds must be subject to prudential supervision. Consumers (i.e. future pensioners) must be protected in an area where they have little knowledge. Supervision must ensure that fund managers execute their fiduciary duties correctly. The regulatory approaches towards pension funds differ widely between Member States. In some states they are covered by regulations specific to pension funds; in others, they are regulated on the same footing as life insurance companies. This means they are subject to the same minimum solvency requirements, rules as to technical provisions and investment restrictions and other provisions as life insurance companies.
36. Whilst national regulations differ, there are commonalities in approach.
    - A requirement for pension funds to be authorised or approved by a competent authority.
    - Authorisation or approval could be dependent on fulfilling certain criteria, such as the suitability and approval of managers of pension funds and custodians/depositaries/trustees of the funds' assets; the legal form of the fund.
    - A requirement for prudential supervision of the fund, including regular reporting rules and powers of intervention by the supervisory authority.
    - Minimum prudential rules on the investment of members' contributions, in particular requiring that they be invested prudently.

Question: Do interested parties agree that these points provide an appropriate basis of regulation?

B. The Effect of Excessive Rules on Pillar 2 Pension Fund Investments

37. There are no specific EU harmonization rules relating to the investment by pension funds of their assets beyond the principle of, and general rules relating to, the free movement of capital.[21] These are intended to guarantee to all investors, including pension schemes, the freedom to invest where they wish in the EU. The

[21] Art. 73b of the Treaty.

Treaty permits[22] investment restrictions to be imposed if these can be justified on prudential grounds. Member States may not use this exception to the freedom as a means of discriminating against foreign assets, nor as disguised, non-prudential restrictions introduced for other reasons. Further, the Treaty prohibits[23] any 'privileged access' by central, regional or local government to financial institutions, including pension funds, through the imposition of minimum investment requirements, except on prudential grounds. The Commission is in the process of taking action against Member States that discriminate for non-prudential reasons against foreign assets.

38. Many Member States have restrictive rules that generally fix the maximum percentage of a fund that can be held in a particular asset or currency (see Table IX [see p. 135 below]). Germany is an example of such an approach. It fixes the following maximum asset levels: 30% equity, of which a maximum of 6% may be non-EU equities, 25% EU property, 6% non-EU bonds, 20% overall foreign assets and 10% self-investment limit. Pension funds in Member States with such quantitative rules tend to hold a high proportion of assets in government bonds.

39. Member States' rules defining the appropriate supervision can have the effect of frustrating the Single Market and the investment advantages it can bring. The Commission believes that in many cases they go beyond what is objectively necessary to maintain adequate prudential supervision. There are other prudential rules and techniques that are consistent with a Single Market and maintain equivalent prudential security. In particular, Member States' prudential rules relating to investment portfolios can have the effect of obliging pension and life insurance funds to invest a large proportion of their assets in domestic government bonds. Even so the actual investment pattern of investment by pension funds in several Member States has in effect not reached the limits fixed by the rules. For example in Germany pension funds only invest 6% in foreign assets (maximum allowed 20%) and 11% in equities (maximum allowed 30%).[24]

---

[22] Art 73d 1(b).

[23] Art 104a.

[24] Of course individual pension funds may be constrained by the maximum rules even if on average for all funds the limits are not reached. Some funds may be very "conservative" in their investment strategy and wish to keep a high proportion of government bonds. Other funds with a profile of young members may wish to take a higher proportion of equities.

Question: *The Commission would like to know how far quantitative restrictions limit in fact the investment strategy of pension funds, particularly in Member States where the maximum permitted proportion of equities is not reached.*

Will these restrictions begin to have a greater impact on investment policy if, as is predicted, funds available for investment increase considerably in the future and the opportunity for investment in government bonds is restricted by lack of supply?

40. In the past the Commission has twice put forward a specific interpretation of the Treaty rules for pension funds: first, in a draft Directive[25] that was withdrawn because the amendments proposed by Member States would have legitimised restrictions on pension funds rather than liberalised them; secondly, in a Communication,[26] which was annulled recently by the European Court of Justice on the basis that the Commission intended to impose new binding obligations on Member States.[27]

The Commission believes the objectives of the withdrawn Directive and the Communication still need to be pursued, in a broader context: in fact all the more so in view of the increasing awareness of the need to reform pension systems with a view to ensuring their sustainability. These policy objectives may be summarised as follows:

- freedom for fund managers who are authorised in accordance with the Investment Services Directive, the Second Banking Directive or the Third Life Insurance Directive[28] to offer services all over the EU;
- freedom to invest assets of pension funds under the "prudent man" principle; diversification of assets, including diversification into assets denominated in currencies other than that in which the liabilities of the institution are established; removal of any requirements on pension funds to invest in or refrain from investing in particular categories of assets, nor to localise their assets in a particular Member State, otherwise than on justified prudential grounds. Any restrictions imposed on prudential grounds must be proportional to the objectives they may legitimately pursue.[29]

41. It is not anticipated that removing restrictions would open the

---

25 OJ 93/C 171/11.

26 OJ 94/C 360/08.

27 Case no. C-57/95 France v Commission.

28 Investment Services Directive 93/22/EEC; Second Banking Directive 89/646/EEC; Third Life Insurance Directive 92/96/EEC.

29 The Commission suggested in its draft Directive and Communication as a first step that currency matching requirements should not exceed 60%. In any case the introduction of the EURO will reduce the constraining effect of any currency matching requirements.

floodgates to an alternative style of fund management. Fund managers would take time to adapt to a new investment strategy; in addition, there is evidence of home country bias as well as the normal prudential policy of keeping the bulk of assets in the same currency as the liabilities. Thus despite the absence of restrictions on foreign equity investment, the proportion of such investment is only around 25%-30% in those Member States with the most liberal investment regimes. A further observation in this context is that fund managers very often do not currently take advantage of the investment freedom they do have, so a rush towards equities appears unlikely.

Question: *Do interested parties agree that the approach to EU supervisory rules described above could provide adequate prudential security at the same time as offering the advantages of the prospect of higher returns within the framework of a real Single Market for pension funds?*

C. Rules on Pillar 3 Life Assurance Investments

42. In contrast to pillar 2 schemes, where there is no specific EU harmonisation, the rules for pillar 3 life insurance schemes are harmonised under the Single Market provisions.[30] Once a life insurance company is authorised and supervised in one Member State, it effectively has a European passport and can sell its products in other Member States. A level playing field for competition between insurance companies in different Member States is established and consumers are protected.
43. The relevant EU rules for investment by life insurance companies are given in Table X [see p. 136 below].[31] Of particular significance are the following:
    - investment shall be based on the prudent man principle;
    - Member States may not require insurance companies to invest in particular categories of assets, and
    - Member States cannot oblige an insurance company to keep more than 80% of its assets in a currency matching its liabilities.

    A minority of Member States have a flexible approach to supervision, and insurance companies in such Member States hold a high proportion of assets in equities, including foreign equities.

---

30 Third Life Directive, 92/96/EEC.

31 These provisions concern the EU prudential rules for investments made by life assurance companies, i.e. the assets side of the balance sheet. On the liabilities side of the balance sheet there are also harmonised EU rules. These are based on the calculation of "technical provisions" which are the expected liabilities, and the assets that must back these provisions to ensure the liabilities can be covered. In addition insurance companies are obliged to keep a "solvency margin" of 4% own capital to cover unexpected circumstances and give added assurance that liabilities can be met.

Most Member States however adopt a quantitative approach to supervision, similar to the approach they follow in respect of pillar 2 pension funds (see Table XI [see p. 137 below]). In fact in such Member States most insurance company assets are kept in domestic fixed income securities (Germany 75%, Spain 55%, France 68% and Italy 70%), despite the scope under the rules to invest in equities and foreign assets (equities or bonds, for example) to a greater extent.

Question: *The Commission would like to know how far life insurance funds in Member States that impose quantitative limits are in fact restricted or are likely to be restricted in the future in their investment strategy by national rules. It also asks whether the quantitative limits imposed by Member States should be changed along the lines described in section B for pillar 2 schemes.*

D. Should There be Similar EU Rules for Pillar 2 and 3 Schemes?

44. This Green Paper has examined the prudential rules concerning the investments made by pension and life assurance funds (i.e. the assets side of the balance sheet).The question also arises as to whether pension funds should be subject to rules similar to those that exist for life assurance on the liabilities side of the balance sheet – in particular is there a need to harmonise the technical provisions and the 4% solvency margin of own funds.[32] This is especially the case where they are in direct competition, in particular where employers use life assurance companies to provide employment related pensions (pillar 2) in the form of "group schemes" which are subject to the harmonised rules for pillar 3 schemes[33] (see Table XII [see p. 137 below]).

As regards this point, the organisation representing European insurers (Comité Européen des Assurances – CEA) argues that pillar 2 pension schemes should be subject to equivalent prudential rules whether they are managed or operated by a pension fund or life insurer. The Commission considers there are four options:

- **Option I:** make funds of pillar 2 schemes subject to the rules currently applied to group life schemes;
- **Option II:** adapt the current rules on the solvency margin for group life schemes to the framework currently applied to pillar 2;
- **Option III:** define new common EU standards for both pillar 2 schemes and group life assurance. The Commission would be

---

[32] See footnote 30.

[33] See Third Life Directive 92/96/EEC, and also Ch. II para 28 above.

interested to hear any concrete suggestions;

- **Option IV:** accept the differences that currently exist because de facto they do not lead to significant distortions of competition.

Question: *Before making up its mind the Commission seeks the view of interested parties.*

E. FUND MANAGERS

45. Authorised fund managers are already entitled to sell investment services throughout the EU on the basis of the Treaty as well as of harmonised criteria.[34] These fund managers are also entitled to offer their services to manage pension funds across borders. Restrictions on this freedom can act as a barrier to improving returns on investments, and infringe Treaty freedoms relating to the free provision of investment management services in the Single Market.[35]
46. Efficient management of a pension portfolio implies an appropriately diversified investment strategy, which can require external specialised advice. Pension schemes need to be able to call on advice and management services from the most appropriate source, which might be from a manager established in another Member State. A fund manager in another Member State might be more aware of non-domestic investment opportunities both within the EU and outside it. There should be no impediment to a pension scheme's ability to call on such services. The Commission also considers that increased competition could lead to lower management charges or more efficient management of these funds. Even a one percentage point annual cost advantage or efficiency gain over a working life is an enormous saving.

Question: *The Commission seeks views on this point, and asks also whether any current impediments provide actual barriers to the cross-border provision of services by pension fund managers.*

F. THE WAY FORWARD

47. This Green Paper has suggested that changes may be desirable to the rules governing the prudential supervision of pension and life insurance funds. If it is decided to make these changes the question

---

[34] Second Banking Directive 89/646/EEC; Third Life Insurance Directive 92/96/EEC; Investment Services Directive 93/22/EEC.

[35] Article 59.

arises as to the most efficient instrument to carry them out. There are several possibilities.

Option 1. Rely on Introduction of Euro

This option would reduce the impact of currency matching requirements for participating Member States. Any assets in a participating Member State would automatically be in a matched currency. Such an approach requires no additional legislative or enforcement effort on the part of the Commission. However this approach would not solve the problem of any unjustified quantitative rules that limit investment in certain classes of assets (e.g. equities) so de facto obliging investors to buy (government) bonds. It would not help solve the problem for funds located in Member States not participating in the euro with either currency matching or quantitative limits. However, this approach could be combined with the second option.

In parallel to the introduction of the euro Member States might also make unilateral changes to their national regulations in order to facilitate more efficient pension fund management. Such changes would be a matter for Member States, and would depend on their perceptions about what is appropriate for their particular situation.

Option 2. Apply Current Treaty Freedoms

This option would rely simply on the obligations created by the current Treaty freedoms relating to movement of capital and to the provision of services. The Commission could issue guidelines as to how it interpreted these basic freedoms for the investment of pension and life insurance funds and fund managers to offer their services. It would then examine for each Member State both its general rules and decisions in individual cases, to see if they were justified on prudential grounds. Where the rules or decisions were not justified, the Commission would be obliged to start infringement proceedings under the Treaty. The case law would then develop to show the practical interpretation of Treaty rules. Such an approach however has certain disadvantages:

- it would take time for the practical application of the basic legal principles to become clear;
- it could lead to legal uncertainty. This is particularly so because case law could easily identify clearly abusive cases but would have greater difficulty in deciding marginal cases where the border between justified and unjustified prudential restraints is not a simple bright-line test;

- there is a risk that interpretation derived from case law, which is based on an adversarial procedure in individual cases, would become rigid. It might not allow for sufficient change and flexibility in the rapidly evolving and technical area of financial supervision.

OPTION 3. ADOPTION OF A DIRECTIVE

An alternative approach would be harmonisation by a Directive setting out basic principles. It would allow the interpretation of Treaty provisions in this technical financial area to be worked out in cooperation with all partners. A Directive could incorporate mechanisms for cooperation between the Commission and national supervisors to interpret, and update in line with changing circumstances, the practical application of basic Treaty freedoms for the supervision of pension and life insurance funds. The publication of an opinion, arising from such co-operation, on interpretation and application of the Directives could lead to transparency and certainty. This approach has been tried before, unsuccessfully. The difficulties of obtaining a consensus between Member States on Community legislation in this area are clear; it is possible that the heightened interest in the role of funded supplementary schemes might lead to a greater consensus.

Question: The Commission seeks the views of interested parties.

Chapter IV: Facilitating the Free Movement of Workers

A. General Considerations

48. Article 51 of the EU Treaty requires Community legislation to be adopted in order to remove all barriers in the sphere of social security which impede a genuinely free movement of workers.

On the basis of this Article,[36] the Community has already adopted legislation (Regulations 1408/71 and 574/72[37]), which removes obstacles to cross-border mobility of workers in the field of statutory pensions. This legislation does not apply to supplementary pension schemes.

More and more qualified and highly qualified people make use of their right to free movement. For this category of people, supplementary pension schemes contribute substantially to their social protection.

B. Obstacles to Free Movement of Persons Relating to Supplementary Pensions

49. In its Communication of July 1991,[38] the Commission started a discussion at Community level, on the role of supplementary pension schemes and their impact on free movement.

As a follow up to this communication, the Commission services have explored on several occasions, in conjunction with the representatives of Member States, Social Partners and pension funds, how to remove obstacles to cross-border mobility of employed and self-employed persons in the European Union in the field of supplementary pensions.

Given the specific nature of many supplementary pension schemes and their extreme diversity at national level as regards their origin, their occupational and material scope, as well as their legal and technical forms, the current coordination system created for statutory schemes does not seem to be the appropriate instrument to address the problems. A more flexible approach is required.

---

36 Since the extension in 1982 of its personal scope to self-employed persons, Regulation 1408/71 is based on Articles 51 *and* 235.

37 Lastly amended and updated by Regulation (EC/118/97; O.J. of L28 of 30 January 1997).

38 Communication of the Commission to the Council, "Supplementary social security schemes: the place of supplementary pension schemes in the social protection of workers and their effect on the free movement" SEC(91)1332.

50. In February 1996 the Commission decided to ask a High Level Panel on Free Movement of Persons chaired by Mme Veil to deliver an opinion inter alia on the measures to be taken in order to eliminate the obstacles to freedom of movement of workers which arise in the context of supplementary pensions.

The panel presented its report in November 1996. It came to the conclusion that legislative action at Community level is necessary but that it should be confined, at least initially, to a three-pronged approach, encompassing the following elements:

a) Preservation of acquired rights for members who cease active membership of a supplementary pension scheme as a consequence of moving from one Member State to another at least to the same extent as for members ceasing membership of the scheme but remaining within the Member State in question.

This specific point is inspired by a basic principle of Community law, namely that of "equal treatment". This means that a worker who leaves a supplementary pension scheme in order to work for another employer in another Member State should not lose the rights already acquired in the first scheme which he would have had preserved had he/she changed employer while remaining in the same Member State.

b) Cross-border payments: Member States should ensure the application of another fundamental principle of the Treaty (free movement of capital and payments) by taking measures in order to permit payments in other Member States of all benefits due under supplementary schemes.

c) Measures allowing workers temporarily seconded by their employer in another Member State to remain affiliated to the supplementary pension scheme in the country in which they were previously working. To this effect all obstacles to cross-border affiliation should be eliminated.

As a first step towards dealing with the obstacles to free movement arising in the area of supplementary pensions, the Commission intends very soon to present a proposal for a Directive concerning the aspects highlighted by the High Level Panel's report. This has already been announced in the Commission's Communication on improving social protection in the European Union.

51. The Commission is also considering the usefulness of establishing a Community Pensions Forum, as suggested by the High Level Panel. This Forum would be constituted by representatives of the Member States, the Social Partners and pension funds. Its purpose would be to explore the possibilities for solving the outstanding problems for mobility in the context of occupational pensions. For instance, by bringing together the different interest groups, it could serve to find solutions to the problem of non-recognition of pension schemes as between the Member States. In general, its task would be to advise the Commission on the best way to overcome the remaining obstacles to free movement.

52. As has been indicated above, there remain, however, a number of obstacles to free movement, other than those which will be dealt with by the proposal for a Directive. The problems identified can be summarised as follows:
- burdensome qualifying conditions for acquiring supplementary pension rights, including long vesting periods;
- difficulties with transferability of vested pension rights from one Member State to another;
- tax difficulties linked to acquiring pension rights in more than one Member State;
- the specific disadvantage of changing schemes arising in the case of a worker other than a seconded worker who goes to work only temporarily in a Member State other than that in which he/she has been building up pension rights.

53. *Qualifying conditions for acquiring rights*

The acquisition of vested rights often takes place after several years of employment in a company (ten years under German law) and sometimes only at the time of retirement. Any job change before the acquisition of a vested right implies that no occupational pension will be paid in respect of this period of employment. Some pension schemes cover however all employees of a given industry (e.g. construction industry). In this case job changes within the industry and within a given country will not be penalised by the loss of pension rights. Cross-border job changes, however, do involve a switch to a new pension scheme. This can therefore be considered as an obstacle to the cross-border mobility of labour.

54. The reason for this is the negative impact on free movement of lengthy vesting periods, either because a worker hesitates to leave his original employer for fear of losing the rights he/she has been building up, or because he/she is reluctant to move to a Member State where lengthy vesting periods are the rule because it will take too long to build up the right to a pension. For example, an Italian or Spanish migrant worker in Germany may have to stay 10 years with the same employer in order to obtain an acquired right under an occupational pension scheme in this country.

55. *Difficulties with transferability of vested pension rights from one Member State to another including the lack of approved mechanisms for recognising pension funds*

On the question of transferability, there are at present obstacles to transferring acquired rights to a scheme in a Member State other than that in which they have been constituted. These obstacles may take the form of legal regulations or of scheme rules.

If a job leaver has obtained a vested right it will be necessary to decide what to do with this right. Two possibilities exist: rights can be preserved in the pension scheme in which they were acquired, and the job leaver will be able to draw a pension from this scheme once he/she retires. The alternative, if the nature of the scheme allows, is to pay out a capital value representing vested rights. This capital value can then be used to buy a deferred annuity from an insurance company or be paid into the new pension scheme, provided of course the new scheme accepts the transfer.

56. Capital transfer seems to be a straightforward solution in the case of funded pension schemes, but is not normally used in the case of book reserve plans and pay-as-you-go schemes, neither of which set aside financial assets to back up their pension promises. Many job changers therefore have only one option, i.e. that of preserving their rights in the previous pension scheme.[39] In either case – transfer or preservation – future pay rises will not normally be taken into account as they would be after an uninterrupted career with the same employer. Frequently, not even expected price or average earnings rises are taken into account for the calculation of transfer values. As a result, there is a tendency for scheme leavers not to get their fair share out of a pension fund.

Calculation of transfer values which penalise scheme leavers and inadequate preservation of "dormant" rights are severe obstacles to labour mobility.

57. *Tax difficulties linked to acquiring pension rights in more than one Member State*

Although direct taxation is largely within the competence of the Member States, Member States must exercise their powers consistently with Community law.[40] In this regard, it should be noted that Article 48 implies not only the abolition of any discrimination based on nationality but also the suppression of any national measure likely to impede or render less attractive the exercise, by Community nationals, of the fundamental freedoms guaranteed by the Treaty.[41] Chapter VI below deals more generally with taxation issues.

Workers who wish to exercise their right to free movement within the Union may come up against tax obstacles when trying to transfer accrued benefits (where this is possible) from a funded scheme in the home state to a scheme in the host state. The transfer from the home state scheme may be subject to a tax charge; this can lead to tax disadvantages where the host state does not give tax relief for the incoming transfer, but the benefits are ultimately received subject to income tax. This illustrates the unfavourable position that workers exercising their right of free movement can

[39] This would also be the case if the new employment relationship did not provide for membership in an occupational pension scheme.

[40] See *Finanzamt Köln-Altstadt* v. *Schumacker*, Case C-279/93, judgment of 14 February 1995.

[41] See *Kraus*, Case C-19/92, ECR [1993] I-1663, judgment of 31 March 1993.

find themselves in by comparison with those who transfer accrued benefits within a Member State.

58. *The specific disadvantage of changing schemes arising in the case of a worker who goes to work for a short term period in a Member State other than that in which he has been building up pension rights*

Two situations can be distinguished:

- Workers seconded by their employers to another country in the context of the same company or associated companies: this situation will be dealt with by the proposal for a Directive, which is mentioned above.
- All other workers moving for a limited period to another Member State: These workers, as much as seconded workers, are disadvantaged by changing pension schemes. This constitutes a discouragement of free movement of labour across Member States' boundaries.

C. Possible Approaches

59. One question which has been raised is whether it would be feasible to deal only with the obstacles encountered in the context of compulsory schemes, as opposed to voluntary schemes. It is argued that a regulatory initiative applying to voluntary schemes would act as a disincentive to employers who would otherwise choose to establish such schemes. It seems difficult, however, to treat differently regimes which, so far as the worker is concerned, have the same purpose of completing his or her pension provision. To exclude voluntary systems would have very different effects according to the Member State concerned.
60. From the consultations carried out, it appears that a particular problem arises in relation to any proposal of limitation, imposed by Community legislation, of the length of vesting periods. However, lengthy vesting periods whatever their advantages in other areas may be, constitute obstacles to free movement; so it is necessary to consider how this problem might be overcome. This could be done by legislation at Community level, which would impose a maximum number of years by way of vesting periods. It could also be specified that no Member State could increase the length of existing vesting periods. Another option could be that the Community should not propose anything by way of legislation in this area, and should rather limit itself to promoting the debate at European level by the social partners.
61. On the question of transferability, the approach discussed with Member States and social partners so far is to require that transferability should be allowed where the nature of the scheme permits (typically, funded systems). In other cases, preservation

would be the only option. It could also be required that the amount transferred be given a fair actuarial valuation, both by the transferring scheme and the scheme receiving the worker.

In order to resolve technical problems relating to the transferability of pension rights such as the transfer of rights only to approved supplementary pension schemes or the establishment of actuarial standards of transfer values, the creation of a Community Pension Forum, as suggested by the High Level panel, made up of representatives of Member States, the Social Partners and Pension funds, could be useful.

62. In order to remove tax disadvantages, Member States could be encouraged to include specific provisions on the tax treatment to be given to contributions, transfer values and benefits in their bilateral double taxation treaties. Although this would allow individual agreements to be adapted to the specificities of the tax systems concerned, agreeing specific provisions in all the bilateral treaties would be a lengthy and cumbersome process. It would also be less transparent than having common rules at Community level, although such rules might be difficult to negotiate.

63. The proposal for a Directive as referred to above will in principle contain measures allowing workers temporarily seconded by their employer in another Member State to remain affiliated to the supplementary pension scheme in the State in which they were previously working.

This possibility of trans-border affiliation could be extended to all workers moving for a limited period to another Member State. This would require an agreement between the employer in the State of origin, the employer in the Host Member State, the worker, and, where applicable, the supplementary pension scheme in question.

Questions: *1. Is action at Community level required in order to overcome the identified obstacles to free movement (i.e. other than those which will be dealt with in the forthcoming proposal for a directive) in the field of supplementary pensions?*

2. If so, which action would be the most appropriate for each of the identified remaining obstacles (legislation, agreement between social partners)?

3. If not, how could the remaining identified obstacles to free movement be removed?

4. Which further initiatives should the Commission take in order to remove the remaining obstacles to free movement?

Chapter V: The Importance of Taxation for Supplementary Pensions

A. General Considerations

64. The taxation of retirement provision is of particular importance in the design of any funded supplementary scheme, and most, if not all, Member States give some form of tax privilege. The design of pension schemes and the choice between different models of taxation are, however, essentially a matter for Member States. Each national government must decide which tax environment will be most effective for its circumstances, bearing in mind the exchequer costs of giving reliefs. The tax rules which have been developed over many years are extremely complex and specific to each Member State. They contain detailed regulations whose purpose is to ensure that government income that is foregone to encourage saving for retirement is used only for that purpose.
65. This diversity leads to a situation where taxation can be a barrier to free movement of people and the free provision of services. Tax privilege usually depends upon a scheme meeting a number of detailed rules, and, as a consequence, a scheme that is approved in one Member State is very unlikely to meet the tax requirements for schemes in another. This has the practical effect of discouraging contributions to pension funds established in other Member States.
66. Within this framework, the Commission is concerned that any specific tax rules should be consistent with the fundamental Community principles of freedom of movement of persons and of provision of services. This applies both to pillar 2 and pillar 3 pension arrangements. For pillar 3 arrangements the Third Life Directive now provides for the free provision of services in the EU, on the basis of home state supervision. The removal of supervisory barriers to cross-border business by insurance companies has, however, highlighted some tax disadvantages which can occur, particularly in relation to the tax deductibility of life assurance premiums.
67. Tax rules that discriminate against a policyholder who buys a policy from an insurer established in another Member State run contrary to the freedom to provide services. In its decision in the *Bachmann* case[42] however, the European Court of Justice held that such discriminatory provisions might be retained to the extent that they are necessary to preserve the particular coherence of the tax system of a Member State. In this case the ECJ upheld a provision of Belgian tax law whereby premium relief for life assurance

[42] *Bachmann* v. *Belgium, Commission* v. *Belgium* (C204/90 and C300/90, judgment of 28 January 1992).

contracts was only permitted in respect of policies issued by companies established in Belgium. The reason was that relief on premiums was linked to taxation of the policy proceeds; if relief were given on premium payments made to foreign insurers, the Belgian tax authorities would not be certain that tax would ultimately be paid on the proceeds.

68. In a later case the Court has made it clear that fiscal coherence could not be invoked as a justification in circumstances where a Member State had voluntarily given up that coherence, for example in the provisions of a double taxation treaty with another Member State. The judgment in the *Wielockx* case[43] shows that a Member State should take into account the effect that double taxation agreements might have on the fiscal coherence that the particular measure creates at a national level. If under the terms of a double taxation treaty a Member State allows benefits paid to non-residents to be taxed only in the country of their residence, the inability to tax these payments should not be a reason for denying tax deductibility only when the contributions are paid to a scheme that is established elsewhere in the Community.

B. Avoiding Double Taxation

69. Each Member State has entered into a large number of double taxation agreements with other states, both within the Union and outside. These treaties, which are nearly all bilateral in nature, are designed to promote economic activity by removing the possibility of double taxation, while at the same time ensuring co-operation to combat tax evasion and fraud. Within the Union, 98 of the 105 possible bilateral relations are currently covered by such a double taxation agreement. Where no bilateral treaty exists, some Member States allow relief from double taxation on a unilateral basis.

70. When it comes to the taxation of occupational pensions, existing agreements tend almost exclusively to concentrate on eliminating the double taxation of pensions when they are paid. Most bilateral treaties follow Article 18 of the OECD Model Treaty in giving the country in which the taxpayer resides the exclusive right to tax pension income from a private employment. (On the other hand, pensions for public service are covered by Article 19 of the OECD Model, and are generally taxed in the country in which they originate.) Even though some recent bilateral tax agreements give taxing rights over pensions from private employment to the source country, the essential principle of preventing double taxation holds good. In this way, the same income will not be taxed twice.

71. A few bilateral agreements between Member States, such as the ones between France and the UK and between Denmark and the

[43] Case C-80/94, judgment of 11 August 1995.

UK, specifically cater for pension contributions which a migrant worker may continue to pay to a scheme in one country after moving to the other. These provisions, which go beyond the scope of the OECD Model, essentially provide for a form of mutual recognition of tax-approved pension schemes in the other country. This has the result of allowing the migrating worker to continue to get tax relief in his or her new country of residence on pension contributions paid to the former one. These steps can result in the lifting of barriers to mobility of workers.

C. The Case for a Common Approach

72. Bilateral double taxation agreements have the considerable advantage that they can be tailored to the specificities of the taxation and the pensions systems of the two countries concerned. Against this, however, must be set the relatively cumbersome nature of the system in that, for relations within the Union, it is clearly time consuming to have to negotiate and renegotiate 105 agreements. This number can be expected to rise sharply with the prospect of future enlargement.[44] Finally, there is no general knowledge of these agreements, and no equality of treatment of equivalent situations under different bilateral agreements.
73. Closer co-ordination of the cross-border tax treatment of pensions could, however, substantially streamline the process of updating, and possibly extending, the scope of bilateral tax agreements. Such co-ordination seems particularly suited to the needs of a developing Single Market, and could be effected in a number of ways. As a first step, it would be necessary to consider whether any specific initiatives or measures are called for by the particular Union context. If Member State governments agreed any rules, there would then be a choice of how to implement them: they might, as now, be incorporated in individual agreements between Member States; or, alternatively, they could be implemented on a multilateral basis. It may on the other hand be appropriate for an agreement on certain aspects of pension taxation to be enacted as Community legislation.
74. In particular, given the need to ensure that the tax benefits that are accorded to pension schemes are not misused, there will also be a continuing need for rules against tax avoidance. With this in mind, there appears to be particular merit in exploring the concept of mutual recognition of tax-approved schemes in other Member States, as already exists in a few bilateral double taxation treaties. Such an approach, for example in the area of cross-border contributions, could prevent retirement tax reliefs from being

44 It would, for example, require 190 agreements to cover all bilateral relations within a Union of 20 Member States.

misused for other purposes.

75. The Commission's report of 22 October 1996 on the development of tax systems[45] stresses the need to view taxation policy in the context of the major political challenges that are currently facing the European Union. Chief among these are the themes of promoting enterprise and employment.[46] The Commission's report, which reflects and draws conclusions from the work of the High Level Group on Taxation,[47] underlines its belief that, in order to harvest the full benefits of the Single Market and to stimulate enterprise, tax obstacles and disadvantages to doing business within the Union must be tackled head on.

76. The Commission's report notes the taxation of pensions as a possible area for a future initiative at Community level, and also that, in the High Level Group, many personal representatives called for action to improve the functioning of bilateral double taxation treaties. While fully bearing in mind the principles of subsidiarity and proportionality, the Commission considers that it may prove most useful to explore ways of improving the co-ordination and scope at Community level of tax rules relating to pension provision. Such rules would, of course, be subject to unanimous decision in the Council.

77. The previous chapter discussed the particular concerns associated with workers temporarily employed in a Member State other than their home state, and the legislation which the Commission intends to put forward. This proposal provides an opportunity to take a small but significant step towards coordinating certain taxation provisions, at least in the specific area of supplementary pensions.

Questions: *To what extent do current tax rules or regulations (for example, related to membership of approved schemes) constitute an actual barrier to the freedom of movement of workers?*

Is it feasible to rely on bilateral or multilateral tax treaties to take forward closer co-operation between Member States as regards cross border pension arrangements? If so, what should these cover, and how can this co-operation be achieved practically?

Is Community legislation an appropriate and feasible alternative?

---

45 Com (96) 546.Final.

46 Florence European Council 21-22 June 1996. Presidency Conclusions (SN300/96) pages 2-3.

47 This High Level Group, under the chairmanship of Commissioner Monti, brought together personal representatives of EU finance ministers on four occasions between June and October 1996, following the informal ECOFIN meeting on 13 April 1996.

Tables

General comment: Given the growing economic importance of funded pension schemes it is essential for those involved with retirement provision, whether economic operators, public authorities or other interested parties, to have at their disposal reliable and harmonised Community statistics on institutions for retirement provision. Such statistics are to be integrated in the competent Community framework regulation, Council Regulation 58/97, concerning structural business statistics.

Table I: Coverage levels – pillar 2

Country	*Coverage Estimation in % of total private sector employment*	*Characteristics*	*Supplementary pensions as % of total pensions (1993)*
Belgium	31	Voluntary/funded/pension funds and group insurance	8%
Denmark	80	Company funds/professional funds through collective bargaining/all funded	18%
Germany	46	Voluntary/partially book-reserved (approx. 56%) funded (44%) through Pensionkassen, Support Funds and Collective Insurance	11%
Greece	5	Voluntary/mainly top hat/some (limited) funding	n.a.
Spain	15	Voluntary/mainly top hat in view of high levels of social security pensions/partially funded/mainly book reserves: will now be phased out	3%
France	90	Quasi mandatory/collective bargaining/PAYG/plus voluntary top hat funded schemes	21%
Ireland	40	Voluntary/funded/pension funds and group insurance	18%
Italy	5	Voluntary/mainly top hat in view of high levels of social security pensions/partially funded	2%
Luxembourg	30	Voluntary/mainly book reserve type plans/a limited amount of funding exists	not available
The Netherlands	85	Company funds/industry-wide funds through collective bargaining/all funded	32%
Portugal	15	Voluntary/pension plans (not funds) executed by recognised management companies and insurance companies/funded/mainly top hat in view of high levels of social security pensions	not available
UK	48	Voluntary/funded	28%

Source: European Federation for Retirement Provision (EFRP) – European Pension Funds 1996 – based on World Bank Report –Tamburi Report.

Table II: Pension fund assets – total and as a percentage of GDP (1993)

	Assets bn ECU	*Assets in % of GDP*
Belgium	7	3,4
Denmark	26	20,1
Germany[1]	106	5,8
Spain	10	2,2
France	41	3,4
Ireland	18	40,1
Italy	12	1,2
The Netherlands	261	88,5
UK	717	79,4
EU[2]	1198	20,3
US	3546	59,1
Japan	1800	44,7

Source: EFRP – *op. cit.*

[1] Book reserves in Germany: 124 bn ECU (1992) source CEA.
[2] EU total includes only Member States listed.

Table III: Assets of life assurance companies – total and as a percentage of GDP (1995)

Country	*Life assurance enterprises assets bn ECU)*	*Assets as % of GDP*
Belgium	6	2,9
Denmark	65	49
Germany	379	20,5
Greece	n.a.	
Spain	18	4,2
France	317	30,0
Ireland	n.a.	
Italy	31	3,7
Luxembourg	5	37,6
Netherlands	138	45,6
Austria	5	1,7
Portugal	3	3,9
Finland	6	6,3
Sweden	65	36,9
UK	565	67,1
EUR 15	1604	24,9

Note: Figures not completely comparable, owing to different national valuation rules (investments can be valued at purchase price, as in Germany, or at current price, as in the UK). EU total included only Member States listed.
Source: Eurostat 1997

Table IV: Distribution of pension funds (pillar 2) assets, as a percentage of total assets (1994)

	Equity	*Fixed income*	*Real estate*	*Short term placements*	*% of Foreign assets*
Belgium	36	47	7	10	n.a.
Denmark	22	65	9	4	7
Germany	11	75	11	3	6
Spain	4	82	1	13	5
France	14	39	7	40	5
Ireland	55	35	6	4	n.a.
Italy	14	72	10	5	5
Netherlands	30	58	10	2	25
Portugal	(18)	(57)	5	19	n.a.
Sweden	32	47	8	13	12
UK	80	11	6	3	30
US	(52)	(36)	4	8	10
Japan	(29)	(63)	3	5	n.a.

Source: Royal Institute of International Affairs, UBS and EFRP (figures between brackets are estimates)

Table V: Distribution of life assurance assets (pillar 3) as a percentage of total assets (1994)

COUNTRY	*EQUITIES*		*FIXED INCOME*		*REAL ESTATE*	*OTHER*
	Domestic	*Foreign*	*Domestic*	*Foreign*		
Denmark	20	5	66	–	3	6
Germany*	5	n.a.	76[2]	n.a.	5	14
Spain*	2	n.a.	55	n.a.	10	33
France	19	–	69	–	8	4
Italy	7	5	70	5	12	2
Nether-lands	12	2	71[1]	4	6	6
Sweden*	23	n.a.	61	n.a.	7	9
UK	49	12	24	3	9	3

* denotes countries where split between domestic and foreign assets was unavailable
[1] includes loans (50%)
[2] includes loans (61%)
Sources: Comité Européen des Assurances, OECD Insurance Statistics Yearbook 1987-1994

Table VI: Differences in rates of return of equities compared to bonds

The period over which the differences in rates of return of equities compared to bonds is calculated is important. The premium normally associated with the returns on equities over bonds depends very much on the level of the stock market and the beginning and end of the period over which comparisons are made. Several different sources are given below. Whilst the difference varies, all sources show consistently the higher return on equities.

Table VIa: Real rates of return (% pa) (1967-1990) in domestic currency

Country	*Equities*	*Bonds*
Denmark	7,0	3,4
Germany	9,5	2,7
France	9,4	1,0
Italy	4,0	-0,2
Netherlands	7,9	1,0
Sweden	8,4	-0,9
UK	8,1	-0,5
US	4,7	-0,5
Japan	10,9	0,2

Source: E.P. Davis: 1995

Table VIb: Excess returns of equities over bonds markets (% pa) (1981-1995) in domestic currency

Belgium	11,5
Germany	7,1
France	4,5
Italy	1,5
Netherlands	6,9
Sweden	15,5
UK	2,9
Japan	2,9
US	1,5

Source: JP Morgan; FT/S+P Actions World Indices; Pragma Consulting

Table VIc: Real returns, USA, UK, Belgium

Real returns (% pa) from US markets (1926-1984)	
Small company stocks	9,1
Large company stocks	7,1
Long term govt. bonds	1,7

Real returns (% pa) from UK market (1919-1993)	
Equities	7,9
Gilts (long)	2,0

Real returns (% pa) from Belgian market (1959-1994)	
Equities	4,6
Fixed income	2,3

Source: Ibbotson Associates Inc.; BZW 1994; Banque Degroof

Table VII: Pension funds 1984-1993 Average rates of return, volatility and relationship of return to risk

	Average nominal Pension Fund Return (real returns in brackets)	*Average Standard Deviation of nominal returns*	*Return/risk ratio[3] on nominal returns (Col 1 ÷ Col 2)*
Belgium	11,8 (8,8)	8,9	1,3
Denmark	10,0 (6,3)	9,4	1,1
Germany	9,4 (7,1)	7,2	1,3
Spain	13,8 (7,0)	19,9	0,7
Ireland	14,0 (10,3)	13,7	1,1
Netherlands	9,5 (7,7)	7,2	1,3
Sweden	14,5 (8,1)	8,5	1,7
UK	15,5 (10,2)	11,4	1,4
US	13,5 (9,7)	9,4	1,4
Switzerland	7,6 (4,4)	6,7	1,1
Japan	8,2 (6,5)	8,3	1,0

Source: EFRP
Note: Similar figures on the returns on life insurance investments will shortly be available through EUROSTAT within the framework of Insurance Service Statistics.

[3] The higher the better.

Table VIII: Stock markets' size (domestic equity) (1996)

Country	*Market capitalization in % of GDP*
Belgium	45.9
Denmark	41.8
Germany	29.6
Greece	19.7
Spain	42.3
France	38.9
Ireland	49.7
Italy	21.7
Luxembourg	193.4
Netherlands	97.8
Austria	14.3
Portugal	23.7
Finland	50.7
Sweden	97.2
UK	149.9
EU	32
US	68
Japan	65

Source: Federation of European Stock Exchanges and European Commission

Table IX: Summary of national regulations on pension fund portfolios (pillar 2)

Country	*Restrictions*
Denmark	A maximum of 40% may be invested in "high risk assets" – these include domestic equities, foreign equities and unlisted securities. Also 80% currency matching requirement. In case of EU currency, up to 50% of liabilities can be covered by assets denominated in ECU. No self-investment.
Germany	Maximum 30% EU equity, 25% EU property, 6% non-EU shares, 6% non-EU bonds, 20% overall foreign assets, 10% self-investment limit[4]
Spain	5% limit in securities issued by any one enterprise. 90% of assets must be invested in quoted securities, bank deposits, property or mortgages. 1% must be in current accounts or money market.
France	At least 50% to be invested in EU government bonds, less than 33% in loans to sponsors.
Italy	No pension law for self-administered schemes but investment policy determined by the board of directors and usually restricted to government bonds, bank deposits, insurance policies and property.
Netherlands	5% self-investment limit; prudent man rule.
Sweden	Majority to be held in bonds, debentures and loans.
UK	5% self-investment limit; prudent man rule.
USA	Prudent man rule.
Japan	Minimum 50% in bonds, maximum 30% equity, 20% property, 30% foreign, 10% in one.

Source: European Commission "Supplementary Pensions in the European Union" (1994)

[4] This does not apply to book reserve schemes.

Table X: EU rules on investment by life insurance companies (pillar 3)

The EU rules on investments by life insurance companies may be summarised as follows (Articles 20 ff and Annex I of 3rd Life Directive):

- investment must take account of the type of business carried on by an undertaking in such a way as to secure the safety, yield and marketability of its investments, which the undertaking shall ensure are diversified and adequately spread ("prudent man");
- the types of assets that can be used to cover technical provisions (basically future claims/pension payouts) are specified (equities, bonds, etc.);
- the method of valuing these assets is specified;
- Member States may not require insurance companies to invest in particular categories of assets;
- in addition Member States shall require every assurance undertaking to invest, with respect to its technical provisions, no more than:
  - 10% in any one piece of land or building;
  - 5% in shares or bonds of the same undertaking except those to a State, regional or local authority;
  - 5% in unsecured loans including 1% for any single unsecured loan;
  - 3% cash in hand;
  - 10% in shares not dealt in on a regulated market, and
- finally Member States cannot oblige an insurance undertaking to keep more than 80% of its assets in a currency matching its liabilities.[5]

[5] Assets denominated in ECU are deemed to be matched.

Table XI: Summary of national regulation of life assurance companies (pillar 3)

Country	*Restrictions*
Denmark	40% combined limit on domestic equity and foreign equity, 10% limit on unlisted securities, 10% combined limit on mortgages and loans.
Germany	Maximum 30% domestic equity, 25% property, 6% foreign equity, 5% foreign bonds, 10% unlisted securities, 50% combined limit for mortgages and loans.
Spain	No specific limits.
France	65% combined limit on domestic equity, unlisted securities and foreign equity. 40% limit on property, 10% combined limit on mortgages and loans.
Italy	Maximum: 20% domestic equity, 20% unlisted securities, 20% foreign equity, 50% foreign bonds, 50% property, 50% mortgages, 0% loans.
Netherlands	10% combined limit on unlisted securities and mortgages, 8% limit on loans.
Sweden	25% combined limit on domestic equity, unlisted securities and foreign equity. 25% combined limit on property and mortgages, 10% limit on loans.
UK	10% combined limit on unlisted securities, mortgages and loans.

Source: Policy Issues in Insurance, OECD, 1996

Table XII: Assets of group life schemes as a percentage of pillar 2 pensions assets (1994)

Country	%
Belgium	73
Germany[6]	12
Spain	52
France[7]	6
Netherlands	25
Finland	56
Sweden	81
UK	5
EU[8]	

Source: CEA

6 Bulk (56%) of assets of pension funds are book reserves.

7 Group life premia as a percentage of total pension premia. Assets could not be calculated in view of fact that main pension schemes (AGIRC/ARRCO) are on a PAYG basis.

8 Includes only listed Member States and excludes France.

Table XIII: Pension funds v. life insurance

Similarities exist between pension funds and certain life insurance products: both aim at provision of a sum at a future date and are often granted tax inducements to encourage such provision. In some states this outward similarity is reflected by the application to pension funds of the regulations similar to those that apply to life insurance under the Third Life Directive. The principal similarities and differences are listed below.

Similarities:

- Both are long term investments.
- Both involve professional management of assets through authorised persons.
- The interests of consumers are crucial in both 'products'.
- Both therefore entail standards to avoid unnecessary risk to the funds entrusted by the consumer to the manager/company.

Differences:

- Pension scheme liabilities are longer term than life insurance liabilities. The average for life assurance contracts is around 8-12 years. For pensions, liabilities are very often in the region of 20-25 years; more, if the pension benefits are paid from the same source. This suggests that pension funds need to match their longer term liabilities with longer term assets. This tends to lead towards a higher proportion of equity or property investment than is the case for life assurance.
- Life policies are subject to the risk of early surrender. This requires appropriate provisioning in the form of readily liquidable assets, or cash, in order to meet expected, and unexpected, levels of early encashment. By contrast, regulations generally prevent early surrender of pension funds benefits, except in very limited circumstances. In addition, transfers to other schemes may be permitted only in certain circumstances, for example on a change of job, and this will generally result in a penalty. The level of short term liquidity requirement is therefore much lower for pensions.
- Similar points can be made in connection with loans. Life insurance companies generally offer loans on the security of life policies. They need to ensure short term liquid assets exist to provide these loans. Pension schemes cannot usually offer such a facility; therefore short term liquidity for this purpose is not necessary.
- Life insurance liabilities are generally expressed in nominal terms: there is a given sum assured, fixed at the outset of the policy. In contrast, pension liabilities are linked to salaries – in which case what is important is real growth. Purchasing shorter term assets in respect of long term pension liabilities could be dangerous, as there is a strong risk that those assets will not achieve a level of growth sufficient to maintain the pension expectations of scheme members.
- In defined benefit schemes an important factor is the 'guarantee' provided by the employer that the pension promise will be honoured whatever the investment return on the fund. No such guarantee exists in the context of life insurance. This guarantee can obviously affect the attitude to investment of the fund manager.

Appendix B: Council Directive 98/49/EC of 29 June 1998 on Safeguarding the Supplementary Pension Rights of Employed and Self-Employed Persons Moving Within the Community

Text

COUNCIL DIRECTIVE 98/49/EC of 29 June 1998 on safeguarding the supplementary pension rights of employed and self-employed persons moving within the Community

THE COUNCIL OF THE EUROPEAN UNION,

Having regard to the Treaty establishing the European Community, and in particular Articles 51 and 235 thereof,

Having regard to the proposal from the Commission,[1]

Having regard to the opinion of the European Parliament,[2]

Having regard to the opinion of the Economic and Social Committee[3],

(1) Whereas one of the fundamental freedoms of the Community is the free movement of persons; whereas the Treaty provides that the Council shall, acting unanimously, adopt such measures in the field of social security as are necessary to provide freedom of movement of workers;

(2) Whereas the social protection of workers is ensured by statutory social security schemes complemented by supplementary social security schemes;

(3) Whereas the legislation already adopted by the Council with a view to protecting the social security rights of workers moving within the Community and of members of their family, namely Council Regulations

[1] OJ C 5, 9.1.1998, p. 4.
[2] OJ C 152, 18.5.1998.
[3] OJ C 157, 25.5.1998, p. 26.

(EEC) No 1408/71 of 14 June 1971 on the application of social security schemes to employed persons, to self-employed persons and to members of their families moving within the Community[4] and (EEC) No 574/72 of 21 March 1972 laying down the procedure for implementing Regulation (EEC) No 1408/71 on the application of social security schemes to employed persons, to self-employed persons and to members of their families moving within the Community,[5] concern only statutory pension schemes; whereas the system of coordination provided for in those Regulations does not extend to supplementary pension schemes, except for schemes which are covered by the term 'legislation' as defined by the first subparagraph of Article 1(j) of Regulation (EEC) No 1408/71 or in respect of which a Member State makes a declaration under that Article;

(4) Whereas the Council has a wide discretion regarding the choice of the most appropriate measures for attaining the objective of Article 51 of the Treaty; and whereas the system of coordination provided for in Regulations (EEC) No 1408/71 and (EEC) No 574/72, and in particular the rules of aggregation, are not appropriate to supplementary pension schemes, except for schemes which are covered by the term 'legislation' as defined by the first subparagraph of Article 1(j) of Regulation (EEC) No 1408/71 or in respect of which a Member State makes a declaration under that Article, and should therefore be subject to specific measures, of which this Directive is the first, in order to take account of their special nature and characteristics and the diversity of such schemes within and between Member States;

(5) Whereas no pension or benefit should be subject to both the provisions of this Directive and those of Regulations (EEC) No 1408/71 and (EEC) No 574/72, and therefore any supplementary pension scheme which comes within the scope of those Regulations, because a Member State has made a declaration to that effect under Article 1(j) of Regulation (EEC) No 1408/71, cannot be subject to the provisions of this Directive;

(6) Whereas in its Recommendation 92/442/EEC of 27 July 1992 on the convergence of social protection objectives and policies[6] the Council recommended that Member States should 'promote, where necessary, changes to the conditions governing the acquisition of pension and, especially, supplementary pension rights with a view to eliminating obstacles to the mobility of employed workers';

(7) Whereas a contribution to this objective can be made if workers who move or whose place of employment moves from one Member State to another are guaranteed equal treatment as regards the protection of their supplementary pension rights with workers who remain or whose place of employment changes but remains within the same Member State;

[4] OJ L 149, 5.7.1971, p. 2. Regulation as last amended by Regulation (EC) No 1223/98 (OJ L 168, 13.6.1998, p. 1).

[5] OJ L 74, 27.3.1972, p. 1. Regulation as last amended by Regulation (EC) No 1223/98 (OJ L 68, 13.6.1998, p. 1).

[6] OJ L 245, 26.8.1992, p. 49

(8) Whereas freedom of movement for persons, which is one of the basic rights enshrined in the Treaty, is not confined to employed persons but also extends to self-employed persons;

(9) Whereas the Treaty does not provide powers other than those of Article 235 to take appropriate measures within the field of social security for self-employed persons;

(10) Whereas, in order to enable the right of free movement to be exercised effectively, workers and others holding entitlement should have certain guarantees for equal treatment regarding the preservation of their vested pension rights deriving from supplementary pension schemes;

(11) Whereas the Member States should take the necessary measures to ensure that benefits under supplementary pension schemes are paid to members and former members thereof as well as others holding entitlement under such schemes in all Member States, given that all restrictions on the free movement of payments and capital are prohibited under Article 73b of the Treaty;

(12) Whereas in order to facilitate the exercise of the right to free movement, national regulations should, where necessary, be adjusted in order to enable contributions to continue to be made to a supplementary pension scheme established in one Member State by or on behalf of workers who are posted to another Member State in accordance with Title II of Regulation (EEC) No 1408/71;

(13) Whereas in this regard the Treaty requires not only the abolition of any discrimination based on nationality between workers of the Member States but also the elimination of any national measure likely to impede or render less attractive for those workers the exercise of the fundamental freedoms guaranteed by the Treaty as interpreted by the Court of Justice of the European Communities in successive judgments;

(14) Whereas workers exercising their right to free movement should be adequately informed by employers, trustees or others responsible for the management of supplementary pension schemes, particularly with regard to the choices and alternatives available to them;

(15) Whereas this Directive is without prejudice to the laws of the Member States concerning collective action to defend the interests of trades and professions;

(16) Whereas, by reason of the diversity of supplementary social security schemes, the Community should lay down only a general framework of objectives and therefore a Directive is the appropriate legal instrument;

(17) Whereas, in accordance with the principles of subsidiarity and proportionality as set out in Article 3b of the Treaty, the objectives of this Directive cannot be sufficiently achieved by the Member States and can therefore be better achieved by the Community; whereas this Directive does not go beyond what is necessary to achieve those objectives,

HAS ADOPTED THIS DIRECTIVE:

Chapter I Objective and Scope

ARTICLE 1

The aim of this Directive is to protect the rights of members of supplementary pension schemes who move from one Member State to another, thereby contributing to the removal of obstacles to the free movement of employed and self-employed persons within the Community. Such protection refers to pension rights under both voluntary and compulsory supplementary pension schemes, with the exception of schemes covered by Regulation (EEC) No 1408/71.

ARTICLE 2

This Directive shall apply to members of supplementary pension schemes and others holding entitlement under such schemes who have acquired or are in the process of acquiring rights in one or more Member States.

Chapter II Definitions

ARTICLE 3

For the purpose of this Directive:

(a) 'supplementary pension' means retirement pensions and, where provided for by the rules of a supplementary pension scheme established in conformity with national legislation and practice, invalidity and survivors' benefits, intended to supplement or replace those provided in respect of the same contingencies by statutory social security schemes;

(b) 'supplementary pension scheme' means any occupational pension scheme established in conformity with national legislation and practice such as a group insurance contract or pay-as-you-go scheme agreed by one or more branches or sectors, funded scheme or pension promise backed by book reserves, or any collective or other comparable arrangement intended to provide a supplementary pension for employed or self-employed persons;

(c) 'pension rights' means any benefits to which scheme members and others holding entitlement are entitled under the rules of a supplementary pension scheme and, where applicable, under national legislation;

Chapter III Measures for Safeguarding the Supplementary Pension Rights of Workers Moving Within the Community

ARTICLE 4 EQUALITY OF TREATMENT AS REGARDS PRESERVATION OF PENSION RIGHTS

Member States shall take the necessary measures to ensure the preservation of vested pension rights for members of a supplementary pension scheme in respect of whom contributions are no longer being made to that scheme as a consequence of their moving from one Member State to another, to the same extent as for members in respect of whom contributions are no longer being made but who remain within the same Member State. This Article shall also apply to other persons holding entitlement under the rules of the supplementary pension scheme in question.

ARTICLE 5 CROSS BORDER PAYMENTS

Member States shall ensure that, in respect of members of supplementary pension schemes, as well as others holding entitlement under such schemes, supplementary pension schemes make payment in other Member States, net of any taxes and transaction charges which may be applicable, of all benefits due under such schemes.

ARTICLE 6 CONTRIBUTIONS TO SUPPLEMENTARY PENSION SCHEMES BY AND ON BEHALF OF POSTED WORKERS

1. Member States shall adopt such measures as are necessary to enable contributions to continue to be made to a supplementary pension scheme established in a Member State by or on behalf of a posted worker who is a member of such a scheme during the period of his or her posting in another Member State.
2. Where, pursuant to paragraph 1, contributions continue to be made to a supplementary pension scheme in one Member State, the posted worker and, where applicable, his employer shall be exempted from any obligation to make contributions to a supplementary pension scheme in another Member State.

ARTICLE 7 INFORMATION TO SCHEME MEMBERS

Member States shall take measures to ensure that employers, trustees or others responsible for the management of supplementary pension schemes provide adequate information to scheme members, when they move to another Member State, as to their pension rights and the choices which are available to them under the scheme. Such information shall at least correspond to information given to scheme members in respect of whom contributions cease to be made but who remain within the same Member State.

Chapter IV Final Provisions

ARTICLE 8

Member States may provide that the provisions of Article 6 shall apply only to postings that commence on or after 25 July 2001.

ARTICLE 9

Member States shall introduce into their national legal systems such measures as are necessary to enable all persons who consider themselves wronged by failure to apply the provisions of this Directive to pursue their claims by judicial process after possible recourse to other competent authorities.

ARTICLE 10

1. Member States shall bring into force the laws, regulations and administrative provisions necessary to comply with this Directive not later than 36 months following the date of its entry into force, or shall ensure by that date at the latest that management and labour introduce the requisite provisions by way of agreement. Member States shall take all necessary steps to enable themselves at all times to guarantee the results imposed by this Directive. They shall immediately inform the Commission thereof.

When Member States adopt these provisions, these shall contain a reference to this Directive or shall be accompanied by such reference at the time of their official publication. The procedure for such reference shall be adopted by Member States.

They shall inform the Commission of the national authorities to be contacted regarding the application of this Directive.

2. Not later than 25 January 2002 Member States shall communicate to the Commission the text of the provisions of national law which they adopt in the field covered by this Directive.

3. On the basis of the information supplied by Member States, the Commission shall submit a report to the European Parliament, the Council and the Economic and Social Committee, within six years of the entry into force of this Directive.

The report shall deal with the application of this Directive and shall, where appropriate, propose any amendments that may prove necessary.

ARTICLE 11

This Directive shall enter into force on the day of its publication in the Official Journal of the European Communities.

ARTICLE 12

This Directive is addressed to the Member States.

Done at Luxembourg, 29 June 1998.
For the Council
The President
R. COOK

www.ingramcontent.com/pod-product-compliance
Lightning Source LLC
Chambersburg PA
CBHW071344230926
51846CB00002B/447